Leaders of Black Civil Rights

Other Books in the History Makers Series:

Leaders of Black Civil Rights

By Marjorie Vernell

Lucent Books
P.O. Box 289011, San Diego, CA 92198-9011

On Cover: A. Philip Randolf (top left), Thurgood Marshall (center), Martin Luther King Jr. (top right), Myrlie Evers-Williams (bottom right), Malcom X (bottom left).

Library of Congress Cataloging-in-Publication Data

Vernell, Marjorie, 1948–
    Leaders of black civil rights / by Marjorie Vernell.
      p.   cm. — (History makers)
    Includes bibliographical references and index.
    Summary: Discusses seven leaders of the Civil Rights movement.
Including Thurgood Marshall, Martin Luther King Jr., and Malcom X.
    ISBN 1-56006-670-9 (lib. bdg. : alk. paper)
      1. Afro–American civil rights workers—Juvenile literature.
2. Afro–American leadership—History 20th century Juvenile literature.
3. Afro–American Civil rights—History Juvenile literature. 4. Civil rights
movements—United States—History 20th century Juvenile literature. 5.
United States—Race relations Juvenile literature. [1. Civil rights workers.
2. Afro–Americans—Biography. 3. Civil rights movements. 4. Race relations.] I. Title. II. Series.
  E185.61. V47   2000
  323'.092'396073—dc21
[B]   99-39569
                                          CIP

Copyright 2000 by Lucent Books, Inc.
P.O. Box 289011, San Diego, California 92198-9011

Printed in the U.S.A.

CONTENTS

FOREWORD

The literary form most often referred to as "multiple biography" was perfected in the first century A.D. by Plutarch, a perceptive and talented moralist and historian who hailed from the small town of Chaeronea in central Greece. His most famous work, *Parallel Lives*, consists of a long series of biographies of noteworthy ancient Greek and Roman statesmen and military leaders. Frequently, Plutarch compares a famous Greek to a famous Roman, pointing out similarities in personality and achievements. These expertly constructed and very readable tracts provided later historians and others, including playwrights like Shakespeare, with priceless information about prominent ancient personages and also inspired new generations of writers to tackle the multiple biography genre.

The Lucent History Makers series proudly carries on the venerable tradition handed down from Plutarch. Each volume in the series consists of a set of five to eight biographies of important and influential historical figures who were linked together by a common factor. In *Rulers of Ancient Rome*, for example, all the figures were generals, consuls, or emperors of either the Roman Republic or Empire; while the subjects of *Fighters Against American Slavery*, though they lived in different places and times, all shared the same goal, namely the eradication of human servitude. Mindful that politicians and military leaders are not (and never have been) the only people who shape the course of history, the editors of the series have also included representatives from a wide range of endeavors, including scientists, artists, writers, philosophers, religious leaders, and sports figures.

Each book is intended to give a range of figures—some well known, others less known; some who made a great impact on history, others who made only a small impact. For instance, by making Columbus's initial voyage possible, Spain's Queen Isabella I, featured in *Women Leaders of Nations*, helped to open up the New World to exploration and exploitation by the European powers. Unarguably, therefore, she made a major contribution to a series of events that had momentous consequences for the entire world. By contrast, Catherine II, the eighteenth-century Russian queen, and Golda Meir, the modern Israeli prime minister, did not play roles of global impact; however, their policies and actions significantly influenced the historical development of both their own countries and their regional neighbors. Regardless of their relative importance in the greater historical scheme, all of the figures chronicled in the History Makers series made contributions to posterity; and their public achievements, as well as what is known about their private lives, are presented and evaluated in light of the most recent scholarship.

In addition, each volume in the series is documented and substantiated by a wide array of primary and secondary source quotations. The primary source quotes enliven the text by presenting eyewitness views of the times and culture in which each history maker lived; while the secondary source quotes, taken from the works of respected modern scholars, offer expert elaboration and/or critical commentary. Each quote is footnoted, demonstrating to the reader exactly where biographers find their information. The footnotes also provide the reader with the means of conducting additional research. Finally, to further guide and illuminate readers, each volume in the series features photographs, two bibliographies, and a comprehensive index.

The History Makers series provides both students engaged in research and more casual readers with informative, enlightening, and entertaining overviews of individuals from a variety of circumstances, professions, and backgrounds. No doubt all of them, whether loved or hated, benevolent or cruel, constructive or destructive, will remain endlessly fascinating to each new generation seeking to identify the forces that shaped their world.

Seven Who Fought for Civil Rights

The journey of African Americans toward full participation in American society, with rights and privileges equal to those of white Americans, is a long one. At times this quest surged forward; at others, it seemed like a dream that would never come true. The mid–twentieth century was a time of great progress in the fight for civil rights. People who came from humble beginnings combined intelligence and determination to accomplish a purpose greater than mere personal gain.

A. Philip Randolph was one such man. Sometimes called "the Father of the Civil Rights Movement," he understood that black workers needed to band together to win improved pay and working conditions. He struggled in the 1920s and 1930s on behalf of the Brotherhood of Sleeping Car Porters and not only changed their circumstances but also drew attention to the plight of black workers in general. He was the first person to dream of a great protest march on Washington that would demonstrate the desire of black people for the same access to jobs and other economic benefits as whites.

While organizing black workers was one route to change, another was challenging discriminatory laws in the courts. As an attorney for the National Association for the Advancement of Colored People (NAACP), Thurgood Marshall became a leader in the quest to overturn unjust laws that affected the lives of black Americans. His successful argument before the Supreme Court in 1954 that a separate education could never be an equal education convinced the Court to make its historic school desegregation ruling. Marshall went on to become a federal judge and finally the first black U.S. Supreme Court justice.

While some voices spoke in court for change, others rang out from the pulpit. Martin Luther King Jr. combined his great speaking ability and his commitment to nonviolent protest to become one of twentieth-century America's best-known and respected leaders. Through the steady pressure of nonviolent protest, he shifted the focus of blacks' efforts from simple endurance to active challenge of the existing order.

Though most people in what came to be known as the civil rights movement practiced King's philosophy of nonviolent protest to achieve an integrated society, there was a fiery proponent of another point of view. Although he, too, was the son of a minister, Malcolm X drew on his life as a street hustler and a seven-year stay in prison in formulating his philosophy that freedom from economic and political oppression should be achieved by any means necessary, including violence. Rather than looking to integration as the means to achieving equality with whites, Malcolm X worked to develop resources that he believed African Americans already possessed independently of white society. Toward the end of his life, he, too, became interested in working toward goals that furthered equal access for all people to political and economic power.

Thanks to the efforts of civil rights leaders, desegregation took place in schools like this one in Fort Myer, Virginia.

Achieving the right to vote was a big step forward in gaining political power and influence for blacks.

For other civil rights advocates, the ballot box seemed the most powerful tool for achieving equality. Fannie Lou Hamer worked for thirty-eight years in the cotton fields of Mississippi, all the time wondering what she could do to change conditions for herself and those around her. For Hamer, registering to vote seemed the best way to improve the conditions that ruled the lives of poor black people in the South. Hamer, without the benefit of much formal education but with determination, courage, common sense, and intelligence, worked to breach the barriers to black participation in voting and party politics.

Even as some activists worked tirelessly to achieve political power through the vote, others worked to bring economic power to bear on problems faced by African Americans. The Reverend Jesse Jackson, as head of Operation Breadbasket, focused attention on African Americans' need for better jobs. Jackson carried that idea forward by forging agreements with major corporations as well as with local businesses in Chicago to hire more blacks in a variety of positions. Jackson, using the publicity generated by Operation Breadbasket, has built a substantial base of political support. His two attempts to win the Democratic Party's presidential nomination have proved that African Americans can be serious candidates for national office. As he continues to work for political and economic change for all people, Jesse Jackson will likely be a political force in the twenty-first century.

While the ability to wield political power is important, so, too, is the ability to keep African Americans working together to achieve their goals. Myrlie Evers-Williams spent the first part of her adult life as the wife of Medgar Evers, the head of the NAACP in Jackson, Mississippi. She was committed to fighting for black civil rights as much as her husband was, and the two worked as a team in the local NAACP office until the time of his death. In the years since, Evers-Williams has remained a tireless promoter of equal rights. She became an educator as well as a civil rights activist. Her most recent triumph was taking over the direction of the NAACP. During her four years as chair of the organization, she managed to settle the legal problems, erase most of the debt, and revitalize the organization that has for almost a century worked to bring the benefits of being American to everyone.

From the union halls of labor to the halls of the Supreme Court, from the streets of the urban ghetto to the cotton fields of the Mississippi Delta, all of these civil rights leaders committed their lives to something larger than themselves. In doing so, they not only helped their people but also earned the respect of all those who value justice and equality.

CHAPTER 1

A Brief History of the Civil Rights Movement

Historians consider the civil rights movement to have begun in 1954. African Americans had always struggled for their rights, from the fight to free themselves from slavery in the nineteenth century to the demand for equal treatment socially, politically, and economically. However, in the years following World War II, their efforts combined into a coordinated massive appeal for justice.

Racial segregation had been informally in force since the end of slavery and was officially sanctioned by the Supreme Court in its 1896 decision, *Plessy v. Ferguson*. In the South, laws known as "Jim Crow," which officially segregated the white and black populations, affected every area of life. Schools, movies, parks, buses, and even cemeteries had separate sections for whites and "coloreds," as African Americans were sometimes called. Segregationists argued that "separate but equal" was the best way to handle race relations. The concept was a fiction, however, since every accommodation set aside for blacks was unequal to its white counterpart.

An End to Segregated Schools

This inequality of treatment was the basis of Thurgood Marshall's argument to the Supreme Court in 1954 in the case of *Brown v. Board of Education of Topeka, Kansas*. Building upon cases that he had won in the 1930s and 1940s in which black graduate students won acceptance into schools of higher learning, he showed how unequal the schools were and the lasting damage they did to black students. On May 17, 1954, the Supreme Court ruled that racial segregation in public schools was unconstitutional and, therefore, illegal.

Although this was a great victory against segregation, Jim Crow laws did not disappear. What was needed was an event that would focus attention on segregationist policies and on black people's determination to get rid of them. Such an event happened in Mont-

Although segregated schools were officially done away with after Brown v. Board of Education, *overcrowded and poorly supplied black schools still existed in the South.*

gomery, Alabama, between December 5, 1955, and December 20, 1956, when the black population boycotted the city buses, protesting segregated seating.

The Montgomery Bus Boycott

The boycott that began the civil rights movement started when a mild–mannered seamstress, Rosa Parks, was arrested for refusing to give up her seat on a city bus so that a white person could sit down. When Parks was arrested, the black community rose in protest, led by a young Baptist minister named Martin Luther King Jr.

Twenty-six-year-old King took inspiration from the writings of Mahatma Gandhi, who had successfully used nonviolent protests to end British colonial rule in India. King believed that Gandhi's successful tactics, which included mass demonstrations, boycotts, and the purposeful breaking of discriminatory laws, known as "civil disobedience," could be adopted by black people in the United States. King considered nonviolence an effective way for communities to bring about change. Later in his career, he would describe the purpose of nonviolent techniques, writing,

> Nonviolent direct action seeks to create such a crisis and foster such a tension that a community which has constantly

13

refused to negotiate is forced to confront the issue . . . the kind of tension in society that will help men rise from the dark depths of prejudice and racism to the majestic heights of understanding of brotherhood.[1]

In describing the source of King's personal power, University of California professor Cedric J. Robinson writes,

His leadership was grounded on . . . the biblical faith tales retold at thousands of places of worship each Sunday, . . . Afro-Christian hymns, and . . . the Gospel. When he spoke, his speech rhythms and language conspired with beliefs, concepts, ideas, and icons [placed] into Black Christian consciousness for generations.[2]

The vast majority of blacks in Montgomery participated in the boycott. Lack of black ridership caused severe financial losses for the bus company, which finally had to negotiate with the boycott's leaders. Then, in November 1956, the Supreme Court outlawed segregation on Alabama's city buses. The company's policies finally would have to change.

King sought a way to maintain the momentum created by the success of the boycott. Though there already existed organizations

Rosa Parks (center), escorted by Charles D. Langford, her attorney (left), and the local deputy sheriff on her way to the Montgomery, Alabama, city jail.

engaged in the fight for black civil rights, including the National Association for the Advancement of Colored People (NAACP), the Congress of Racial Equality (CORE), and the National Urban League, King gathered a group of black ministers to found the Southern Christian Leadership Conference (SCLC). Its purpose was to organize and focus the black protest movement throughout the South.

Southern whites made no secret of their intention to maintain segregation. In 1957 Arkansas governor Orval Faubus, in defiance of the Supreme Court, forbade the integration of Central High School in the Arkansas capital, Little Rock. Black students faced crowds of angry whites and snarling police dogs as they attempted to enter the school. America watched the events unfold on the television, and suddenly the struggle for civil rights was no longer just a local event. People all over the country had the issue brought before them on a nightly basis.

Black students arrive under military escort for the integration of Central High School in Little Rock, Arkansas.

In 1957 the U.S. Congress passed a new civil rights act, the first such law since 1875. Although it was quite limited, it did allow the federal government to bring civil suits in federal court on behalf of those who were physically threatened or denied their right to vote. The provisions of the Civil Rights Act of 1957 would often be used in the coming years to obtain court orders for local governments to stop discriminatory practices.

As the 1960s opened, the presidential election of 1960 became a key test of African American voting power. The Republican candidate, Richard M. Nixon, was viewed by blacks as favoring continuation of the status quo. African American communities mobilized to vote for John F. Kennedy. In the tight election, their votes were significant.

The new president proved to be sensitive to the needs of this new group of voters. Kennedy appointed a number of blacks to important positions within the government. Likewise, he established the Committee on Equal Employment Opportunity to increase employment of African Americans in federally connected

President John F. Kennedy meets with representatives from the NAACP in 1961.

programs and created the Committee on Equal Opportunity in Housing to prevent discrimination in federally supported housing.

Nonviolent Protests

Following the election of Kennedy, blacks became more assertive in pursuing their goals. A popular method of forcing the desegregation of restaurants became the "sit-in." In one well-known incident, four black students from the Agricultural and Technical College in Greensboro, North Carolina, went shopping in a local variety store and then sat at the store's lunch counter and ordered coffee. The employees refused to serve them. The students refused to leave, remaining until the store closed.

The sit-ins spread rapidly. In many cases, the protesters had foods from the lunch counters thrown on them as they peacefully sat waiting to be served. They sometimes suffered severe beatings by the police who came to remove them. Televised scenes of the abuse heaped on sit-in participants caused a public outcry in other parts of the nation. The protesters themselves took out ads in newspapers like the *Atlanta Constitution* in which they said, "We do not intend to wait placidly for those rights which are already legally and morally ours to be meted out to us one at a time."[3] The protests caused a drop in sales for the affected stores; it became clear that segregation was bad for business. Soon many lunch counters in the South began to serve blacks.

Activities by civil rights organizations surged during the 1960s. CORE organized an interracial group of youthful activists into "Freedom Riders" and sent them south to test segregation laws in interstate transportation. Robert F. Kennedy, by this time the U.S. attorney general, ordered federal troops to protect them from hostile mobs.

Resistance to integration was fierce. Governor Ross Barnett of Mississippi tried unsuccessfully to bar the admission of James Meredith to the University of Mississippi, and Governor George Wallace of Alabama tried to physically block the admission of black students to the University of Alabama. National Guardsmen sworn to enforce federal laws secured the safe admission of the students in both cases.

As it became clear that civil rights would have to be seized by force, pressure mounted on President Kennedy to propose a new federal civil rights bill. The various civil rights organizations acting together decided that a massive show of support was needed for the proposed legislation.

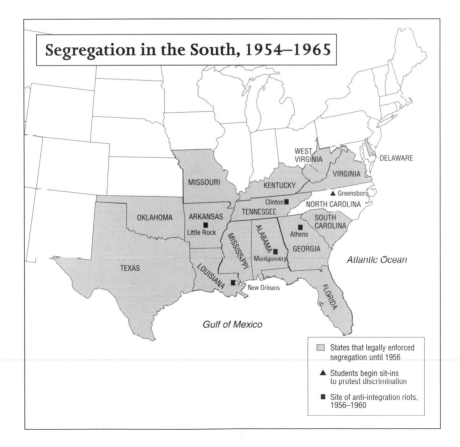

Segregation in the South, 1954–1965

States that legally enforced segregation until 1956

▲ Students begin sit-ins to protest discrimination

■ Site of anti-integration riots, 1956–1960

The March on Washington

On August 28, 1963, as Congress debated the proposed law, some 250,000 Americans gathered in Washington, D.C., to demonstrate their support for the new civil rights bill. A. Philip Randolph, a noted black labor leader and longtime activist, had first proposed such a march in 1941, and now he played a key role in organizing the event. The multitude gathered at the foot of the Lincoln Memorial to listen to a variety of speakers, especially Martin Luther King Jr. After the speakers finished, President Kennedy received civil rights leaders and labor leaders in the White House.

In spite of these efforts, African Americans were disheartened that the legislation languished in Congress. The feelings of discouragement were added to by a series of shocking events. In September in Birmingham, Alabama, members of the Ku Klux Klan (KKK) bombed a black church, killing four black children and sending shock waves through the nation. During the November 1963 elections, numerous southern segregationists were voted into office. Then, on November 22, President John F. Kennedy was assassinated while visiting Dallas, Texas.

Governor George Wallace stands in the door of a building at the University of Alabama to block the integration of that institution.

The Congress of Racial Equality marches in Washington, D.C., in memory of the four children killed in the Birmingham, Alabama, church bombing.

Although the motives of the assassin, Lee Harvey Oswald, had nothing to do with Kennedy's civil rights policies, African American leaders felt that they had lost a great friend. Fortunately his successor, Lyndon B. Johnson, continued the fight for civil rights legislation.

Further progress was apparent when, in January 1964, the Twenty-fourth Amendment to the Constitution was ratified. It outlawed poll taxes, which were fees charged to voters in most southern states. A large portion of the black population of the South earned very little money, so even those who were able to register to vote still could not because they often lacked money to pay this tax. Under the Twenty-fourth Amendment, there was no charge for the right to vote.

The Civil Rights Act of 1964

In July Congress passed the Civil Rights Act of 1964. This law established the Equal Employment Opportunity Commission (EEOC) to be a watchdog over discriminatory employment practices; gave the attorney general additional powers to protect citizens from discrimination; forbade discrimination in most places of public accommodation, such as hotels and restaurants; and extended the life of the Commission on Civil Rights to January 1968.

Southern whites were still not willing to concede and obey the new law. Southern whites responded by boycotting establishments that had integrated their services. Resistance was frequently violent. Black churches, often the center of the black protest movement, were bombed. Three young civil rights workers, James Chaney, Andrew Goodman, and Michael Schwerner, were abducted and killed by the KKK in the summer of 1964.

After President Lyndon Johnson signed the Civil Rights Act of 1964 into law, some white citizens of the South reacted with disobedience and violence.

The Rise of Racial Violence

As whites resisted change, blacks grew frustrated with their nonviolent efforts. Urban riots in the Watts section of Los Angeles in 1965 and in Detroit in 1967 took dozens of lives, injured thousands of others, and caused millions of dollars in property damage.

In part, the riots were a response to the limited economic opportunities in America's cities. The SCLC created Operation Breadbasket to encourage business and economic opportunities for blacks. King felt, moreover, that something had to be done for all poor people in America, regardless of race. To focus attention on the plight of America's poor, King began organizing the Poor People's Campaign. The new effort would include nonviolent demonstrations, nationwide boycotts, and another march on Washington to pressure Congress into backing measures to fight poverty in America.

King's interest in poor working people's struggles drew him to Memphis, Tennessee, in April 1968 to support black sanitation workers who were striking for better pay and the right to form a union. King felt that success in Memphis would give a boost to the Poor People's Campaign. It was in Memphis on April 4, 1968, that Martin Luther King Jr. was assassinated as he stood on the balcony of his motel room.

The death of King touched off an explosion of anger in many of America's cities. To many people, King's death seemed like the final rejection of peaceful tactics. Just two months later, Senator Robert F. Kennedy, who had played such an important role in the early 1960s and was now a candidate for president, was shot and killed as he campaigned for the Democratic Party's presidential nomination. The civil rights movement appeared to have been dealt a crippling blow.

With the death of King, the civil rights movement lost its strongest national leader, but that did not mean an end to African Americans' quest for equality of treatment. Even though it appeared to many that the civil rights movement had ended in 1968, efforts by African Americans to take advantage of gains made in the previous fourteen years continued. The increased influence of black voters led to election of blacks to local, state, and national offices. Blacks became mayors—in some cases of major cities like Los Angeles, Chicago, and Atlanta—and members of their state legislatures. Those elected to the U.S. House of Representatives banded together to form the Congressional Black Caucus, a group that keeps a watchful eye on legislation affecting African American interests.

Looking Ahead

In recent decades increased access to education and equal employment opportunities have improved the economic status of many black people. Although a distressingly high number of African

Martin Luther King Jr. helped organize the historic March on Washington in 1963. Following his death in 1968, other black leaders continued to struggle for equality.

Americans still live in poverty, 61 percent have moved into relative economic stability and sometimes far beyond that. Despite the many problems facing black Americans, the political and educational gains made during the period of the civil rights movement have empowered blacks with more control over their personal fate and their destiny as a people.

As the nation enters the twenty-first century, filled with the promise of new achievements, its African American population looks forward as well. It looks ahead determined to maintain its hard-won freedoms, to resolve the economic crisis that blights the lives of so many youngsters in America's urban centers, and to participate alongside all of the other people of the American mosaic in truly creating the American dream.

CHAPTER 2

A. Philip Randolph: Father of the Civil Rights Movement

On August 28, 1963, a quarter million people from all walks of life peacefully assembled at the foot of the Lincoln Memorial in Washington, D.C., in the largest political demonstration in American history. The March on Washington, as the huge gathering was known, called people from all backgrounds to come to the nation's capital to show their support for the civil rights legislation then under debate in Congress. As the crowds melted away that evening, one lone figure remained standing in the twilight by Lincoln's statue. Tears flowed down his cheeks, for he had seen the fulfillment of an idea he had had some twenty years before. That man, the architect of the March on Washington, was labor leader and longtime civil rights activist A. Philip Randolph.

The Early Years

Asa Philip Randolph was born in Crescent City, Florida, on April 15, 1889. Asa's parents, James and Elizabeth Randolph, named him for a biblical king who sacrificed his personal wealth for the freedom of his people. James Randolph, a minister in the African Methodist Episcopal Church, wanted his sons, Asa and his older brother, James junior, to make notable contributions to their community. Asa's parents loved books and considered education the means for black people to improve their lives.

Getting an Education

Florida in the early twentieth century did not let blacks and whites attend the same schools. Asa and his older brother did not allow segregation to keep them from getting an education, however. At age fourteen he enrolled in the Cookman Institute, a combined high school and junior college in the Jacksonville area.

A. *Philip Randolph poses in front of the Lincoln Memorial in Washington, D.C.*

When he was seventeen, Asa got the chance to spend his summer vacation visiting a cousin in New York City. Life in the big city was quite an experience for a southern boy used to the slow pace of Florida. The streets were filled with activity, noise, jazz, and excitement. Asa loved every minute of his visit.

Even in New York City, segregation was a reality. Although the city was not officially segregated, Asa noticed that there were many places where blacks did not go. Jobs, other than as servants or cleaning people, were not open to blacks. They were able to vote, but their votes seemed to have no effect. However, the opportunity to further one's education did exist. Asa took special note of City College of New York and its wide variety of courses.

Asa returned to Jacksonville, where in 1907 he graduated from the Cookman Institute at the top of his class. Despite his education, the only jobs available to Asa were menial ones. Finally a friend told him of a job as a kitchen helper aboard a boat headed for New York. Asa took the job and left Jacksonville for good.

A New City and New Ideas

Blacks from all over the South were streaming into New York City looking for a better life, settling in an area known as Harlem. It was in this community that Randolph made his home.

Life in the big city suited Randolph. He loved being able to attend City College of New York, where he studied history and economics. He read the works of Karl Marx, the German political philosopher, and agreed with Marx's view that workers were being taken advantage of by the wealthy.

As he studied economics, Randolph also became interested in labor unions as a way of improving conditions for workers, and he began spreading the word about Marx's ideas and about labor unions among the people of Harlem.

Just as had been true in Florida, Randolph found that only menial jobs were open to blacks. He took a job as a waiter on the steamboat *Paul Revere*, which carried passengers between New York and Boston. He found the workers living in cramped, unsanitary conditions and tried to organize them to protest their situation. His activities got him fired, but his efforts were cheered by a group he had joined, the New York Independent Council. This group of activists spent their time helping workers fight the injustices they experienced.

A. Philip Randolph crusaded against the injustices that black workers faced during the early part of the twentieth century.

As he tried to better the lives of his fellow workers, two very important people came into Asa's life. First, he met Lucille Campbell Green, an elegant, intelligent, young black woman who had developed a thriving local beauty business in the building where Randolph lived. Green and Randolph shared many interests, including the theater and concern over improving conditions for black people.

A. *Philip Randolph drew both emotional and financial support from his wife, Lucille Randolph.*

The relationship flourished, and they were married in 1914. Though Lucille found Randolph's ideas extreme, she used the proceeds from her beauty business to support her husband's efforts on behalf of workers. They were dedicated to each other, calling each other "Buddy" to symbolize their close affection for one another.

Lucille introduced her husband to an energetic, quick-witted, young, black man named Chandler Owen, a student at Columbia University. Randolph and Owen became friends and together studied more about socialism. In 1916 the two young men joined the Socialist Party and founded their own organization, the Independent Political Council, to educate people about the causes of poverty.

A Union of Their Own

Randolph and Owen could see that, although unions helped workers, the unions did not allow blacks to join. In response, they decided to organize a union of black workers, starting with elevator operators. Some six hundred men joined the new union, but when asked to go on strike for a small wage increase and a reduction in working hours, the men refused for fear of losing their jobs.

Randolph and Owen decided to take their message about the conditions black workers faced directly to the residents of Harlem. Following a custom in the community, they chose a busy street corner, 135th and Lenox Avenue, to get their message to the local inhabitants. They quickly attracted large crowds of people eager to hear them speak.

The ability of Randolph and Owen to draw large crowds, coupled with their efforts to organize the elevator operators, led to an invitation from a group of waiters who wanted help in publishing a newspaper for restaurant workers. The paper was called the *Hotel Messenger,* and Randolph's job included contributing articles to the paper, which he signed "A. Philip Randolph." One of these articles told about how headwaiters exploited assistant waiters by demanding large sums of money from them for the privilege of working in the restaurant. The headwaiters did not like being exposed and used their influence to have both Randolph and Owen fired from the paper.

The Messenger

Losing their jobs did not stop the young crusaders. They started their own magazine, the *Messenger*. In its pages, Randolph expressed his views on a variety of issues, including his opposition to black participation in World War I.

The *Messenger* soon attracted the attention of the federal government. In June 1917 the U.S. Congress had passed the Espionage Act, which allowed the government to censor what people wrote about the war. This same law made it a crime to advise people not to go into military service. Federal agents raided the *Messenger*'s office as a result of Randolph's outspoken views.

Randolph continued his efforts with the magazine during the 1920s, but he suffered not only from continuing government harassment but also from a lack of interest from the black community. People were becoming more interested in black nationalist

A. Philip Randolph makes a speech at a political rally. Although he went to great lengths to spread his ideas through the nation in the 1920s, most blacks ignored his socialist message.

Marcus Garvey's idea of blacks returning to Africa than in Randolph's message of fighting for civil rights in America. While Randolph opposed returning to Africa, he did think Garvey's ideas served a useful purpose:

> A word about Garveyism to Negroes today. It has done some splendid things. It has inculcated into the minds of Negroes the need and value of organization. . . . It has stimulated the pride of Negroes in Negro history and traditions, thereby helping to break down the slave psychology which throttles and strangles Negro initiative. . . . It has further stiffened the Negro's backbone to resist the encroachments and insults of white people.[4]

As interest in their message dwindled, both Randolph and Owen became disillusioned with the Socialist Party, which paid little attention to the needs of blacks. As Paula F. Pfeffer points out in her biography of Randolph, "Socialists equated racism with the general social problem and told blacks that they would have to wait for the Socialist revolution to achieve complete social equality."[5] Owen quit the party and left New York for Chicago, leaving Randolph alone to ponder his next move.

The Brotherhood of Sleeping Car Porters

Randolph decided that his next move would be to create a newspaper that would appeal to a wider audience than the *Messenger* had. Called the *Black Worker*, this paper attracted the attention of some sleeping-car porters, men who made up the beds on the sleeping cars of passenger trains. They asked Randolph to help them organize a union. Randolph saw one advantage to this situation compared to what the elevator operators faced. Instead of working for many different employers, the porters all worked for the Pullman Company. This meant that a strike would have a major impact on the company.

Though Randolph had quit the Socialist Party, he was still able to gather some ten thousand dollars in donations from Socialists, which enabled him to travel the country to organize the sleeping-car porters. By the end of 1926, Randolph had established locals of the Brotherhood of Sleeping Car Porters from New York to Los Angeles.

At first the Pullman Company refused to take Randolph's efforts seriously, but as the membership in the new organization grew to over seven thousand, company executives reacted. They sent spies to attend union meetings and report on what was said

Members of the Brotherhood of Sleeping Car Porters rallied behind Randolph to organize a strike for improved working conditions.

there. As a result, people who spoke against the company were fired. The company created a newspaper, the *Pullman Porter Messenger*, which spread lies about Randolph and the union organizers, suggesting for instance that they were using union dues for their personal gain.

Randolph's efforts to organize the porters were helped by Congress's passage of the Watson-Parker Act in May 1926. The law protected the rights of railway workers to organize, although it did not force the Pullman Company to negotiate with the union. Finally, Randolph called for a strike vote in 1928. The porters voted in support of a strike, and the attention of the whole nation focused on this group of black workers.

The strike was never to be, however. Although there were many people, black and white, who sympathized with the porters and offered to gather food and clothes for the would-be strikers, the leaders of the American Federation of Labor (AFL) advised Randolph that the porters would surely lose. Unsure of what to do, Randolph called off the strike.

Unfortunately for Randolph, there were those in the African American community who felt that he was a troublemaker. They started an anti-Randolph campaign around the country, spreading the rumor that Randolph had been bought off by the Pullman Company. The porters, feeling betrayed, left the Union in droves. Randolph continued working for the union, and in 1929 the AFL accepted the Brotherhood of Sleeping Car Porters as part of the Hotel and Restaurant Workers Union. Other challenges lay ahead, however.

Help from the Federal Government

As the nation's economy was gripped by the Great Depression in the early 1930s, workers took to the streets to protest government policies. In 1933 Franklin Delano Roosevelt became president. Roosevelt believed that helping workers establish unions would help end the depression by enabling them to bargain for higher wages. New laws like the Emergency Railroad Transportation Act in 1933 and the Railway Labor Act in 1934 limited the ability of companies to force workers to join a company-sponsored union rather than forming their own. In response, Randolph concentrated on rebuilding the Union using the support of the AFL and gathering funds from within the black community.

New legislation enabled Randolph to stage a strike that resulted in large wage increases and less working hours for railway porters.

30

Realizing that company-sponsored unions would never properly represent the workers' needs, the sleeping-car porters began to come back to the Brotherhood of Sleeping Car Porters. Finally, a showdown occurred between the union and the Pullman Porters Protection Association, a group totally sponsored by the Pullman Company. The federal government sponsored an election in June 1935 to see which organization truly represented the porters. Some 8,316 porters voted for the union, and only 1,422 voted for the Pullman-sponsored association.

It was a glorious victory, though it would be another two years before Pullman finally signed an agreement under which the porters got large wage increases and a reduction in work hours from 400 to 240 hours per month.

The Idea of a Great March

By the close of the 1930s, war was raging in Europe. Britain was under attack by Germany, and the United States began sending arms and other goods overseas. As the nation went to work making armaments, Randolph appealed to Congress and the president to forbid defense contractors from discriminating against blacks in hiring. President Roosevelt moved slowly on this issue.

As a means of pressuring the president, Randolph developed the idea of calling a mass gathering of black workers in Washington, D.C. His idea caught fire among black working people. Two months before the July 1, 1941, date of the proposed march, it looked as though there might be as many as one hundred thousand black marchers descending on Washington. President Roosevelt was worried that this march might divide the nation as it was preparing for possible entry into the war. In a concession to Randolph's demands, Roosevelt issued Executive Order 8802, making it illegal for any company receiving federal money to discriminate against blacks. He also established the Fair Employment Practices Committee to enforce his order.

Randolph called off the march on Washington, but he kept the pressure on by holding a series of rallies like the one in Madison Square Garden on June 16, 1942, which was attended by over twenty thousand people. In similar rallies in Chicago and St. Louis, he assured the crowds that efforts to equalize working conditions and opportunities would continue. Addressing the crowd in Chicago, Randolph proclaimed, "Negroes are going to march, and we don't give a damn what happens. . . . Surely Negroes can't be expected to fight for democracy in Burma when they don't have it in Birmingham." [6]

Integrating the Armed Forces

Great challenges lay ahead. As World War II came to an end, most people wanted life to return to normal, the way it had been before the war. However, blacks who had fought bravely on the battlefield and worked hard at home to support the war effort refused to go back to the old ways. One change Randolph had in mind was to end segregation in the military.

Despite the end of World War II, the new president, Harry S Truman, called for the military draft to be reinstated because of what he saw as threats from the Soviet Union. Since the nation's army and navy were both still segregated, Randolph felt that blacks should refuse to be drafted until the military was integrated. He enlisted the aid of Bayard Rustin, the founder of the Congress of Racial Equality, to help organize protests against the peacetime draft.

As a result of pressure from Randolph and other civil rights leaders, President Harry Truman ordered that the armed forces be integrated.

At a hearing before the congressional committee responsible for drawing up the new draft law, Randolph spoke of his opposition to a segregated military in no uncertain terms: "Negroes will not take a Jim Crow draft lying down. . . . I personally will advise Negroes to refuse to fight as slaves for a democracy they cannot possess or enjoy." [7] Finally, on July 26, 1948, Truman signed Executive Order 9981, which ordered the integration of the U.S. military.

Equality for Black Workers

As America moved into the 1950s, Randolph continued to press for equal treatment for black workers, keeping up his efforts to have the AFL treat its black union members fairly. When the AFL joined forces with the Congress of Industrial Organizations (CIO), a labor organization dedicated to organizing workers without regard to race, Randolph felt that he had a chance to accomplish his goal. In 1959 the new AFL-CIO agreed to work harder toward making sure that all workers were treated equally.

Tragedy struck Randolph in March 1963, when Lucille, his wife of forty-nine years, died. Randolph had left his labor organizing and other public duties to remain at Lucille's side during the last months of her life. Upon her death, he was consumed with grief.

The Great March

His longtime associate, Bayard Rustin, wanting to distract Randolph from his grief, began talking with him about organizing a march on Washington to demonstrate for civil rights. Randolph immersed himself in the task. He contacted Martin Luther King of the SCLC and Roy Wilkins of the NAACP about mobilizing one hundred thousand people in support of the civil rights legislation then under consideration by Congress.

President Kennedy was afraid that the march might cause a backlash against the bill by undecided members of Congress. Randolph, on the other hand, felt that delaying the demonstration risked violence:

> The Negroes are already in the streets. . . . If they are bound to be in the streets in any case, is it not better that they be led by organizations dedicated to civil rights and disciplined by struggle rather than to leave them to other leaders who care neither about civil rights nor nonviolence?[8]

On August 28, 1963, the great march took place. The nation had never experienced anything like it. A crowd of 250,000 people gathered peacefully to support the pending civil rights legislation. The first person to speak to the multitude was A. Philip Randolph. The day was a fitting tribute to the man whose efforts on behalf of equal rights for blacks had earned the title "Father of the Civil Rights Movement."

The Last of a Warrior

As the 1960s drew to a close, Randolph saw that his work with the Brotherhood of Sleeping Car Porters was coming to an end. Not only had Randolph grown too old to fulfill his responsibilities as head of the union, but air travel had made the jobs of sleeping-car porters obsolete. Randolph retired in 1968, although he did not become a forgotten figure.

Randolph's lifetime of work in civil rights was honored in 1965 when President Lyndon B. Johnson presented him with the Presidential Medal of Freedom. In 1969, on the occasion of Randolph's eightieth birthday, Governor Nelson Rockefeller of New York declared April 15 "A. Philip Randolph Day."

Randolph remained active in his later years. Through the A. Philip Randolph Institute, he developed an education fund, a youth apprenticeship program, and voter registration and education programs. He was as active in the institute as his health

In his later years, much acclaim was given to Randolph for his efforts on behalf of black workers.

Lyndon Johnson later awarded Randolph the Presidential Medal of Freedom for his efforts to further the cause of black civil rights.

would permit, but advanced age and illness eventually kept him away. On May 16, 1979, just one month after his ninetieth birthday, A. Philip Randolph died.

Today, A. Philip Randolph High School stands on the campus of City College of New York. It is an appropriate way to remember the contributions of one of City College's most famous students, a man who took the ideas learned there and used them to help secure for his people the rights and benefits of a free society.

CHAPTER 3

Thurgood Marshall: A Spokesman for Justice

In the later years of his life, Justice Thurgood Marshall would humorously reflect on his school days in Baltimore during the early twentieth century. In Marshall's recollection, he was a large boy who often disrupted class by arguing with other students and with his teachers. Though the school's principal might have considered using corporal punishment to discipline him, Marshall was too big to whip. So the principal created another punishment: He gave young Thurgood a copy of the U.S. Constitution to memorize and sent him off to the boiler room in the school's basement. Marshall remembers, "If you don't think that's terrible, just try memorizing the Constitution some time." [9]

Thurgood Marshall traced his interest in law back to his childhood, when he was forced to memorize the Constitution.

This early "punishment" was the beginning of Thurgood Marshall's lifelong involvement with the Constitution. Born July 2, 1908, in West Baltimore, Maryland, Marshall was one of two boys born to Norma Arica Marshall and her husband, William Canfield Marshall. The family lived in a respectable middle-class neighborhood called Druid Hill. While his older brother, William Aubrey, had a peaceful disposition, Thurgood became something of a tough guy early in life.

Marshall always liked to claim that his toughness came from his maternal great-grandfather, a slave who was so mean that his master set him free to get rid of him. Marshall's father also was a strong influence, however, teaching his son not to accept racial mistreatment. In addition, his mother, an elementary school teacher, instilled in him a sense of pride in his heritage.

Thurgood, though rowdy and fun-loving, graduated from high school and, like his older brother, went to college. Because blacks at the time were rarely admitted to any of the white colleges in the United States, Thurgood chose to attend Lincoln University, the nation's oldest black college. In 1923 Thurgood Marshall enrolled as a freshman.

College and Law School

Even though he later recalled spending more time having fun than studying, he did maintain a B average. Lincoln University greatly expanded the young man's horizons. Marshall read the works of the influential black authors of the time like W. E. B. Du Bois, Langston Hughes, Jean Toomer, and Countee Cullen. He glimpsed the wider world by associating with classmates such as Kwame Nkrumah and Nnamdi Azikiwe, who would one day become the presidents of their respective countries, Ghana and Nigeria.

During his college days, Marshall discovered that he had a knack for debate. As a member of the university's Forensic Society, he became known as "the Wrathful Marshall," leading his debate team to victory time and again. Although his mother had wanted him to become a dentist, by graduation Marshall had decided on a career in law.

In 1930, while a senior at Lincoln University, Marshall met and married Vivian Burey, nicknamed "Buster," a graduate of the University of Pennsylvania. Marshall's decision to become a lawyer meant that the young couple had to save money, so they moved back to his family's home.

Just as discriminatory admissions policies had affected his choice of college, they also influenced Marshall's choice of law school. The University of Maryland did not admit blacks, so Marshall turned to Howard University in Washington, D.C.

Thurgood Marshall spent much of his school time reading the works of influential authors such as W. E. B. Du Bois (pictured).

Marshall (second row, second from right) resented the policies that barred him from entering the college and law school of his choice.

Though Howard accepted students of all races, it was dedicated to providing higher education for blacks. As it happened, Howard's president, Mordecai Johnson, was in the process of expanding the university's curriculum. Johnson, at the urging of Supreme Court justice Louis Brandeis, had decided to develop a law school so that black lawyers could be trained to protect the constitutional rights of other blacks.

The faculty of the law school included a graduate of Harvard's law school, William Henry Hastie, who would later become the first black person appointed to a federal judgeship, and Charles Hamilton Houston, a lawyer and civil rights activist. Marshall learned how to be a leader from these men, both of whom later became his friends.

Marshall's work with Houston offered him a chance to learn courtroom procedures firsthand. With Houston, he worked to challenge the University of North Carolina in court for refusing law school admission to a black student. Even though he and Houston lost the case, Marshall gained valuable courtroom experience.

Marshall's law school record was so good that he was offered a scholarship to do postgraduate work at Harvard University. Marshall, however, had no intention of becoming a law school professor. He took the bar exam in Maryland and set up a law office in his hometown of Baltimore.

The Freebie Lawyer

In 1933 America was in the midst of the Great Depression, and opening a private law practice in such hard times did not promise to earn Marshall much of a living. Making matters worse, blacks who could afford a lawyer usually went to white lawyers on the

Charles Houston was one of Marshall's professors at Howard University Law School, and he later became a colleague and friend.

assumption that they would somehow get better representation. Marshall was left to represent those who needed help but could not pay. His practice posted a loss of one thousand dollars in its first year, but he persevered, and gradually his list of clients grew.

As more clients began to come to him for help—sometimes referring to him as "the Freebie Lawyer"—he built a name for himself within the black community. In 1934 one of his clients, Carl Murphy, the owner of a local newspaper, along with Lillian Jackson, a housewife, approached Marshall about reviving the local chapter of the National Association for the Advancement of Colored People (NAACP).

A Civil Rights Attorney

Marshall worked hard to build support for the NAACP. He spoke to community groups, went from door to door in every black neighborhood, and put up posters in an effort to organize the black community to combat racism. To provide a focal point around which to rally the community, he called for a boycott of the businesses on Pennsylvania Avenue, a street in Baltimore where blacks shopped in white-owned stores, but where they were

Being a part of the NAACP legal team gave Marshall a focal point for his efforts on behalf of civil rights.

never hired to work. The store owners sued the NAACP, providing Marshall and his former teacher Charles Houston the opportunity to argue the case in court. The NAACP won. The stores on Pennsylvania Avenue could no longer discriminate against blacks in hiring.

Building on this success, Marshall and the NAACP targeted Maryland's individual school boards, suing them for paying black teachers and school principals less than they paid their white counterparts. Over the next several years, Marshall won cases against these school boards, sometimes earning more than a 100 percent increase in pay for his clients.

Through their work, Marshall and the NAACP came to see a need to attack a more basic problem: segregated schools. This would be a harder fight. White resistance to having black and white children attend school together seemed unshakable. Moreover, the Supreme Court's landmark ruling in the case of *Plessy v. Ferguson*, finding "separate but equal" facilities to be legal, appeared firm. Marshall believed, however, that it might be easier to prove that institutions of higher learning could not provide separate but equal education for black students. Marshall and the NAACP targeted law schools, reasoning that judges, also having training as lawyers, would more easily see and understand his arguments and be sympathetic to them.

The first case that Marshall won in this campaign was *Murray v. Pearson* in 1935. Donald Gaines Murray sued the University of Maryland and its president, Raymond A. Pearson, when Murray was refused admission to Maryland's law school and told that he could find equal training in law at Maryland's Princess Anne Academy. The academy offered no courses in law; therefore, Marshall argued that an equal education could not be received at that school.

Over the next several years, Marshall and Houston became a traveling law office, filing successful suits against universities all over the South. This success was bound to get Marshall noticed. By 1936 Marshall had become assistant special counsel for the NAACP's national organization. As assistant special counsel, he handled a case involving Lloyd Gaines, who had applied to the University of Missouri's law school and had been told that the university would pay to send him to school in another state since it could not provide equal facilities. The NAACP argued that Gaines and other black students should not have to leave their home state to receive equal education. The federal court agreed, saying that the state could maintain separate law schools only if

Thurgood Marshall (left) reviews an argument in a lawsuit he brought against the University of Maryland for its practice of segregation.

they were exactly equal. Since it was easier to integrate than to create a new separate-but-equal law school, the university began admitting black students.

Marshall's reputation was growing, but he kept looking for new areas where inequality lurked. One area in which discrimination impacted the lives of black people was in criminal justice. Blacks arrested for crimes against whites were often convicted based on "sunrise confessions"—that is, confessions that the police had beaten out of them during the night. In 1940 Marshall, who by then had replaced the ailing Houston as the NAACP's legal counsel, argued his first case before the Supreme Court, *Chambers v. Florida.* He represented three black men from Florida who had been convicted of murder based on confessions given while they were being beaten by police officers. The Supreme Court overturned the convictions, ruling that the due process clause of the Fourteenth Amendment to the Constitution had been violated. This was the first of Marshall's twenty-seven Supreme Court victories out of the thirty-two cases he would eventually argue there.

Though he continued for a time working to overturn unfair convictions, Marshall gradually turned his attention to voting rights for blacks. For years, southern states had limited black participation in the political process in a number of ways, including controlling who could vote in primary elections. The Democratic Party was dominant in the South at that time, and the party limited its membership to whites. Since only party members were allowed to vote in primary elections, blacks were never able to have a voice in who ran for office as a Democrat. Candidates for other parties rarely had a chance of winning the general election, so the practical effect was to entirely deprive blacks of voting power.

In 1940 Marshall argued before the Supreme Court in the case of Lonnie Smith, a young Texan who had been denied the right to vote in his state's Democratic primary. Basing his argument on the Fifteenth Amendment to the Constitution, which forbids states from denying the right to vote based on race, Marshall won a favorable decision. The high court ruled that blacks could not be prohibited from voting in primary elections.

By this time Marshall was well established as the nation's leading civil rights attorney. Although he had been offered a position in the government as assistant to the solicitor general, Marshall did not accept what looked like an honor. As he later recalled,

Marshall felt he could make his biggest contribution to civil rights in the courtroom.

> When they did give Negroes some jobs in the Roosevelt years, it was always as an assistant to somebody. I remember that when [Francis] Biddle was attorney general, he offered me a job in the Justice Department. I inquired in detail about it. It eventually ended up with me being offered the title of assistant solicitor or something like that. But all I would be doing would be to sign my name to things that were decided and done by somebody else.[10]

The Assault on School Segregation

Once World War II had ended, Marshall found his attention once again focused on the issue of school desegregation. The returning war veterans had education benefits coming to them from the government. Many of these veterans were black, and they found the doors of many colleges closed to them because of their race. Marshall was able to win a number of individual cases against universities, helping blacks to gain admission, but still the Supreme Court was unwilling to completely overturn the *Plessy v. Ferguson* ruling that was the basis for wider segregation.

Marshall still wanted to make an all-out attack on segregated schooling. In the early 1950s he began to review an assortment of cases involving unequal segregated facilities for public-school children. This collection of lawsuits from South Carolina, Delaware, Virginia, the District of Columbia, and Kansas went before the Supreme Court in 1952 under the title of *Brown v. Board of Education of Topeka, Kansas.*

Thurgood Marshall (standing, left) looks on as the dean of admissions of the University of Oklahoma accepts the application of Ava Fisher, the first black student ever enrolled there.

The court listened to three days of arguments in December 1952 but reached no decision. A few months later the plaintiffs and the defendants were asked to come back the following December to deliver further arguments. In the meantime, Marshall and his team picked the brain of every expert available to them. One person in particular had some very important research to share.

Kenneth Clark, an assistant professor of sociology at City College of New York, had done years of studies in which black children were presented with a set of dolls, both black and white. Clark asked the children questions that required them to choose between the dolls. The white dolls were most often chosen by the children, suggesting that the pattern of white preference had been planted in the children's minds, causing them to develop a negative self-image even at an early age.

The proof of emotional and psychological harm caused by segregation, coupled with the proven inequality of the facilities offered to black children, convinced the court that separate schools could never be equal. On May 17, 1954, the Supreme Court ruled that racial segregation in public schools was unconstitutional.

"Mr. Civil Rights"

The school desegregation order knocked a big hole in the stone wall of segregation, but compliance with the law had to be demanded on a case-by-case basis. Marshall, who had tirelessly pursued desegregation, now had new concerns that were far closer to him than his clients: His wife was dying of cancer. She had not told him of her illness, but eventually the symptoms became too obvious to ignore. Marshall spent all of his time with her in the last weeks of her life. She died in February 1955.

Marshall was unprepared for this loss. He had been married for twenty-five years to a woman who had understood and accepted the long hours of work and frequent absences from home that Marshall's job required.

Marshall dealt with his wife's death by rededicating himself to his work for the NAACP. Eventually he began to date a secretary who worked for the organization, Cecilia Suyat. The relationship deepened, and in December 1955 they married. Though Marshall had had no children in his first marriage, Cissy, as she was called, eventually would present him with two sons, Thurgood junior and John William.

Over the next few years, Marshall had his hands full dealing with civil rights cases. From serving as counsel for the nine black

Marshall and his wife Cecilia and two sons at their New York apartment.

students who first desegregated Central High in Little Rock, Arkansas, to protecting the right of the NAACP to continue as an organization in the state of Alabama, Thurgood Marshall was indeed "Mr. Civil Rights."

Then, in 1961, Marshall's career turned in a different direction. President John F. Kennedy nominated Marshall for a judgeship on the U.S. Court of Appeals for the Second Circuit. During the required confirmation hearings by the Senate Judiciary Committee, southern senators subjected Marshall to some of the harshest questioning ever endured by a nominee. The committee finally approved Marshall by a narrow margin, although the entire Senate approved his nomination overwhelmingly.

Marshall soon proved that Kennedy's confidence in him had been well founded. Not one of his decisions was ever overturned by the Supreme Court, a remarkable record and one that only a few other jurists have achieved. Still higher honors awaited him, however.

From Solicitor General to Supreme Court Justice

In 1965 President Lyndon B. Johnson called Marshall to Washington, D.C., to become the solicitor general, whose job it is to represent the U.S. government in federal court cases. The position provided Marshall with the chance to further pursue expansion of civil rights, this time with the backing of the U.S. government.

As solicitor general, Marshall dealt with a number of important civil rights issues, ranging from fair housing in California to voting rights for non-English-speaking citizens. Marshall was also in a position to deliver another blow in support of voting rights by successfully arguing that the state of Virginia's poll tax was violating the Fourteenth Amendment by denying citizens equal protection under the law.

Thurgood Marshall was now nearly sixty years old, but retirement was not in his near future. Within two years, Johnson decided to nominate Marshall to the Supreme Court. Again, the conservatives in the Senate tried to find reasons not to confirm his nomination. Senator Strom Thurmond of South Carolina grilled Marshall on details of post–Civil War constitutional history, which Marshall admitted not knowing. Finally Senator Edward M. Kennedy challenged Thurmond on the same details, forcing him to admit that he could not answer his own questions. Marshall's nomination was confirmed by the Senate, and he became America's first black member of the Supreme Court.

Marshall brought an informal style into the hallowed halls of the Supreme Court. The opinions he wrote were always stated in clear terms easily understood even by people with no legal training.

When Marshall first arrived at the Court, he found himself part of the court's liberal majority. But with the replacement of colleagues like Earl Warren and William O. Douglas with more conservative justices, the court began to slow its expansion of civil rights. Marshall found himself in the minority in decisions on school integration in Detroit (*Milliken v. Bradley*, 1974) and affirmative action in medical school admissions (*Regents of the University of California v. Bakke*, 1978). More and more, he wrote his views as the Court's dissenting opinion.

Marshall's hard work and dedication to the Constitution lead to his appointment as a Supreme Court justice.

Marshall was privately anguished about the conservative turn that the Supreme Court had taken. Although he normally only criticized decisions through his dissenting opinions rather than confronting his collegues directly, on occasion he would make his opinion known in a pointed way. For example, in a 1981 death penalty case, when Justice William H. Rehnquist suggested that the inmate had cost the state too much money with his appeals, Marshall interrupted, saying, "It would have been cheaper to shoot him right after he was arrested, wouldn't it?" [11]

"I Am Getting Old"

As the years wore on, Marshall realized that he was no longer up to the physical demands that being on the Supreme Court placed on him. In 1991 Justice Thurgood Marshall retired from the Court. When reporters asked him why he was stepping down, he said in his typically direct fashion, "I am old. I am getting old and falling apart." [12]

Marshall spoke out in favor of civil liberties right up until his death from heart failure on January 24, 1993. Once asked if Marshall's comments went too far, Justice William Brennan said, "Nothing Thurgood says goes too far for me." [13] It is a fitting tribute to the man who started out as an outspoken boy who was punished by having to memorize the Constitution.

CHAPTER 4

Martin Luther King Jr.: A Nonviolent Warrior

Martin Luther King Jr. was born on January 15, 1929, the first-born son of Reverend Martin Luther King Sr. and his wife, Alberta. The King family lived in Atlanta, Georgia, in a section of town where well-to-do African Americans lived. Martin Luther King Sr. was one of the ministers at the Ebenezer Baptist Church, a church so prosperous that it could afford to employ another minister, King's father-in-law, Reverend Adam Daniel Williams. Williams and his wife lived with the Kings and their three children, Christine, Martin, and Alfred Daniel, in a twelve-room Victorian house a few blocks from the church.

M. L., as young Martin was nicknamed, grew up enjoying the love and support of his family and the members of the Ebenezer Baptist Church. However, M. L. soon became aware that in the American South, life for a young black boy was harsh and threatening. M. L. learned that he could not sit down at a soda fountain, sit where he wanted in a movie theater, or enter places that were marked "Whites Only." M. L. grew up experiencing the injustice that black people suffered, and he wanted to change it.

College Years

King's quick mind allowed him to enter Morehouse College at the age of fifteen. It was at Morehouse that King decided to become a minister after the president of Morehouse, Benjamin Mays, convinced him that ministers had a role to play in helping blacks improve their lot in life.

Armed with this new vision, eighteen-year-old King preached his first sermon to a full house at Ebenezer Baptist Church. The next year, 1948, he was ordained and hired as assistant minister at his father's church. King, however, was not one to settle for a comfortable position when he knew that there was much more he needed to learn. In the fall of 1948, he left Atlanta to attend Crozer Theological Seminary in Chester, Pennsylvania.

This Victorian house was the birthplace and childhood home of Martin Luther King Jr.

Crozer was an exciting place where a student's horizons could expand. There, King continued studying the works of great thinkers, becoming particularly interested in the ideas of Mahatma Gandhi of India.

King learned that Gandhi used nonviolent protest in the form of strikes, boycotts, and marches to free India of British rule. King believed that these same methods could be used to gain civil rights for black people in America.

King graduated from Crozer at the top of his class, but he did not return to Atlanta. He had been accepted into the graduate program in theology at Boston University. In 1951 King headed for Boston, Massachusetts.

It was in Boston that King met Coretta Scott, a young woman from Marion, Alabama. Scott had wanted to become a singer and was not at all sure that she wanted the life of a minister's wife. But finally her love for the handsome young preacher won out, and on June 18, 1953, they were married. The couple continued to live in Boston while King was finishing his doctoral dissertation, and Coretta earned her bachelor of arts degree.

The Kings were in no rush to return to the South. They wanted to raise children where they would receive a better education than they would receive in the segregated schools in the South. However, King's first job offer as a minister, other than in his father's church in Atlanta, was at the Dexter Avenue Baptist Church in Montgomery, Alabama. After much careful thought, the couple decided to move to Montgomery, though they both felt that racial segregation there was even worse than in Atlanta.

Beginnings of Leadership

In 1954 Montgomery had some fifty black churches. King was disappointed, however, when he found that few of the ministers in those churches encouraged their parishioners to work toward an end to segregation.

The year 1955 was an eventful one. In the spring King received his doctoral degree from Boston University. In November of that year, his daughter Yolanda was born. Life was moving swiftly for King. The pace would quicken even more, and his life was about to radically change direction.

The head of the Montgomery chapter of the NAACP, E. D. Nixon, had long wanted to challenge the city ordinance that required blacks to sit in the rear of the city's buses. Since the vast

Dr. Martin Luther King Jr. and his wife, Coretta Scott King.

majority of Montgomery's bus riders were black, Nixon wanted to organize a boycott of the bus company as a way of protesting the treatment of its best customers. All he needed was an incident that would motivate the black community to challenge the existing policy. That incident occurred on December 1, 1955, when Rosa Parks refused to give up her seat so that a white passenger could sit. The police arrested Parks, setting in motion events that would forever change American society.

The Montgomery Bus Boycott

Nixon had spoken to King previously about his plans for a boycott. King called a meeting of black ministers at the Dexter Avenue Baptist Church. Forty-five ministers attended and agreed to announce a boycott from their pulpits on Sunday, December 4. The boycott was planned down to the last detail. To assure maximum participation, King convinced taxicab companies owned by African Americans to offer their services to customers for a dime a ride, the same fare the bus company charged. Once the preparations were complete, King could only pray that the boycott would succeed.

The morning of December 5, 1955, arrived, and, except for eight people, the black population of Montgomery stayed off the buses. Black leaders in the community met that afternoon to discuss ways of building on their success. At that meeting they created the Montgomery Improvement Association (MIA) to coordinate further protests and asked Martin Luther King Jr. to head it.

The boycott lasted almost a year and became a test of wills between the protesters and the city. Montgomery's city council passed an ordinance making it illegal for taxis to charge customers less than forty-five cents for a ride, knowing that blacks could not afford to pay that much on a daily basis. Black residents who owned cars responded by volunteering vehicles to provide carpools. This network of drivers developed a system of pick-up and drop-off points in the black neighborhoods that provided more efficient service than the bus company had.

As the boycott continued, each side took legal action against the other. The MIA sued in federal court to end all bus segregation. The city officials arrested the boycott leaders for breaking an old law that prohibited boycotts, and they threatened to arrest the carpool drivers and have their automobile insurance canceled.

Then, on November 13, 1956, the U.S. Supreme Court declared segregation of buses to be unconstitutional. The black community of Montgomery had achieved a major victory against the unequal treatment that had held them down for so many years. In addition, they had shown that people can overcome their fears and take positive, effective action against oppression without turning to violence. The victory was also a personal one for King. He was no longer just a young minister of a black Southern Baptist church; he was a nationally known figure.

In January 1957 King met with black ministers from ten southern states to form an organization that would coordinate civil rights protest activities throughout the South. The Southern Christian Leadership Conference (SCLC) came into being with King as its leader.

In 1959 King decided that the SCLC should expand its operations and that he should devote all of his time to its leadership. King moved back to Atlanta, where the organization was based, to follow what he saw as his destiny. Even though he knew that being a leader could be dangerous, it was his belief that "the quality, not the longevity, of one's life is what is important." [14]

Peaceful Protests

The peaceful protests that King was advocating spread. On February 1, 1960, four black college students began a sit-in at the lunch counter in the Woolworth's in Greensboro, North Carolina.

King admired the fact that the students were adopting the techniques of nonviolent protest, and he encouraged the students to found their own organization. Known as the Student Nonviolent Coordinating Committee (SNCC), the new organization was given space in the SCLC headquarters.

Not satisfied with merely coordinating the SCLC's activities, King began to take part in sit-ins himself. During one sit-in, King and the other participants were arrested. The local authorities wanted to keep King away from the growing protest movement, so they arranged for him to receive a four-month sentence in a labor camp. King was shackled and taken 250 miles away from Atlanta to Reidsville State Prison.

King, however, had a powerful new ally. Senator John F. Kennedy, the Democratic candidate for president, wanted African Americans to vote for him. Kennedy spoke with the judge who had sentenced King and arranged for King's release. King praised Kennedy publicly for having taken a brave stand against segregation. That November Kennedy received an overwhelming majority of the black vote.

It was soon after Kennedy took office that white and black students began riding buses throughout the South to protest segregation on buses and in bus stations. Calling themselves "Freedom

Riders," they encountered mobs of whites who attacked them and burned their buses. In response to King's demand for help, Robert F. Kennedy, the new attorney general, sent four hundred U.S. marshals to help protect the riders from the mobs.

King now knew that help from the federal government was key to the success of the protests. Wanting to lead a demonstration that the federal government would support and that the media would follow, King decided to focus on Birmingham, Alabama, which was considered to be the most segregated city in America. King had two objectives for the series of demonstrations he planned: He wanted to desegregate the city, and he wanted to pressure President Kennedy into proposing a civil rights bill.

Birmingham offered King an opponent, public safety commissioner Eugene "Bull" Connor, whose temper would surely make him commit acts of violence in front of the television cameras. King held meetings to prepare those who would take part in the protests. The strategy he proposed was that they willingly be arrested in mass numbers in order to fill the jails, thereby putting extra pressure on the local authorities to negotiate with the protesters. When his preparations were complete, King demanded that the city government pass ordinances to desegregate lunch counters, rest rooms, drinking fountains, and other public accommodations. The demonstrations—and the arrests—began.

"Freedom Riders" with their burned bus after an attack by white segregationists.

Martin Luther King Jr. is arrested in Birmingham, Alabama. It was during his stay in jail there that he wrote his most famous letter.

In the Birmingham Jail

King was arrested for leading one march and was taken to jail. It was from there that King wrote one of the most famous documents of the civil rights movement. In his "Letter from Birmingham Jail," King addressed the suggestion by a group of white ministers that he should have waited:

> Frankly, I have yet to engage in a direct action campaign that was well-timed in the view of those who have not suffered from the disease of segregation. . . . I cannot sit idly by in Atlanta and not be concerned about what happens in Birmingham. Injustice anywhere is a threat to justice everywhere.[15]

A few days after the letter was published, King was released from jail. But King had a still-larger protest in mind.

The March on Washington

President Kennedy had submitted civil rights legislation, but it showed no signs of being passed by Congress. King decided that a massive rally in Washington, D.C., was needed. With King's prestige behind it, the march attracted the attention of the nation's television networks.

President John F. Kennedy greets the top civil rights leaders at the White House after the March on Washington.

On August 28, 1963, as the nation watched, 250,000 supporters of civil rights marched from the Washington Monument to the foot of the Lincoln Memorial, where they listened to speeches by such leaders as A. Philip Randolph, U.S. Representative Adam Clayton Powell, and SNCC leader John Lewis. King was the last to speak that day.

He began his speech with the topic of freedom and its long denial to African Americans. As the people responded to his words, King put down his notes and spoke directly to them, emphasizing the need for action:

> It would be fatal for the nation to overlook the urgency of the moment and to underestimate the determination of the Negro. The sweltering summer of the Negro's legitimate discontent will not pass until there is an invigorating autumn of freedom and equality. . . . I have a dream that one day in the red hills of Georgia, the sons of former slaves and the sons of former slaveowners will be able to sit down together at the table of brotherhood.[16]

The phrase *I have a dream* became the powerful central theme of his address. For those assembled at the Lincoln Memorial as well as for the millions watching on television, these four words crystallized the struggle of African Americans.

A crowd of 250,000 stands in front of the Washington Monument to press their demand for racial equality.

A Friend Is Gone

Moving words did not end racial hatred, however, and King knew that much work remained. And that work would have to go on without a longtime friend in the White House. On November 22, 1963, President John F. Kennedy was assassinated. The new president, Lyndon B. Johnson, was a southerner whose position on civil rights was unknown to many.

King hoped that the new president would be a strong supporter of civil rights, and in his first speech to Congress on November 27, Johnson asked Congress to pass the civil rights bill immediately.

After months of delay, Congress did pass the civil rights legislation, and Johnson signed the Civil Rights Act of 1964 on July 2. Although the signing of this act was major proof of the new president's support, King was concerned about some of Johnson's other decisions.

For instance, demonstrations that spring in St. Augustine, Florida, had all ended in police beatings of protesters, whom Johnson chose not to protect with federal troops. King was also concerned that Johnson did not push for the inclusion of more

Martin Luther King Jr. addresses the people during the March on Washington, when he spoke movingly of his dream of equality for all.

black delegates to that summer's Democratic National Convention. Even though King disagreed with the president over these issues, he endorsed Johnson over the Republican candidate, Barry Goldwater, who had opposed passage of the civil rights bill in Congress. Johnson's landslide victory in November suggested that his stance on civil rights had the support of the vast majority of Americans.

The Nobel Peace Prize

King was to receive a different symbol of support for his leadership in civil rights. In December 1964 King received an honor awarded to few people, the Nobel Peace Prize. When he accepted the prize in Oslo, Norway, he said:

> I accept the Nobel Prize for Peace at a moment when 22 million Negroes of the United States of America are engaged in a creative battle to end the long night of racial injustice. I accept this award in behalf of a civil rights movement which is moving with determination and a majestic scorn for risk and danger to establish a reign of freedom and rule of justice.[17]

King returned to the United States with his eyes set on the next prize in the movement: stronger laws protecting voting rights.

Marching from Selma to Montgomery

He chose Selma, Alabama, as the place to begin this new phase of the civil rights struggle. Selma's voter registration office required would-be black voters to take a test on the state's constitution. The questions were so detailed and hard to understand that some could not even be read by the white officials who administered the test. Selma also had a sheriff, James Clark, who was known to be extreme in his treatment of blacks. King knew that the nation and the world would be watching the events in Selma and that the likely confrontations with authorities would generate public support for voting rights.

When members of the black community began trying to register to vote, the local police harassed, beat, and jailed them. In one incident, a young black man named Jimmy Lee Jackson was shot by a state trooper and died seven days later. In response, the SCLC called for a protest march from Selma to Montgomery, a distance of fifty miles.

After two failed attempts, King left Selma leading a group of three thousand people. As they marched through the Alabama

Due in part to his excellent public speaking skills, Martin Luther King Jr. was able to rally thousands in support of voting rights.

countryside, they were joined by people from all over the country. By the time they reached Montgomery five days later, their numbers had swollen to twenty-five thousand.

The march from Selma to Montgomery achieved what King had hoped: The marchers' determination convinced Congress to pass the Voting Rights Act of 1965. Under the new law, all tests that prevented people from registering were banned. The federal government was authorized to help blacks register and oversee federal elections to ensure that everyone could vote freely.

The Movement Changes Focus

Passage of the Voting Rights Act was a major achievement, but much work remained to be done. Racial tension flared in many of the cities of the North and the West. The Watts Riot of August 1965 stunned the nation. Militancy was growing among younger black leaders like Stokely Carmichael of the SNCC and Floyd McKissick of the Congress of Racial Equality. Much to King's dismay, some black leaders favored abandoning nonviolent strategies in favor of more aggressive action.

At the same time, other troubles disturbed America as well. The United States was waging war in Vietnam. Many people believed that America had no business involving itself in a conflict so far from home. King publicly expressed his objections to the war, angering President Johnson. Once sympathetic to King's ideas, Johnson no longer allowed King direct phone access to his office.

Poverty among both blacks and whites was also an increasingly visible problem. King had come to believe that Federal programs to aid the poor were needed. He linked the disastrous war with the continued lack of funding for such programs. In his 1967 book *Where Do We Go from Here?*, King compared the costs of the Vietnam War with what that same amount of money could buy for a poverty-stricken American. King's objections to the war went beyond economics, however. He was also disturbed that so many young black soldiers were being sent to fight for liberties in Vietnam that they did not have in the United States.

Reverend Ralph Abernathy walking with Martin Luther King Jr. as they lead marchers from Selma to Montgomery, Alabama.

The Last Battle

As the 1960s continued, King came to see poverty as America's most pressing problem. He wanted to unite all of the people who had been left out of the American dream. In the spring of 1968, the black garbage collectors of Memphis, Tennessee, were on strike, demanding better wages and working conditions. King traveled to Memphis to help them. To his dismay, a march he led ended in a riot. King felt that he had to lead another march, this time a peaceful one, to compensate.

The plans for the demonstration were painstaking. On the evening of April 4, 1968, after a long day of making the final preparations for the march, King was preparing to go out to dinner. He stepped out onto the balcony of his motel room to shout to his friend Jesse Jackson that he would be right down. A rifle shot rang out, and King fell, mortally wounded by a bullet to the head. The civil rights movement had lost one of its greatest leaders.

The reaction to King's death was swift and violent. Within hours of the news, blacks took to the streets in over one hundred cities around the country. Newspapers and television news programs were filled with dramatic pictures of large sections of cities like Chicago and Washington, D.C., in flames. For a while, it seemed that peace itself had died.

On April 8, 1968, Reverend Ralph Abernathy and Coretta Scott King led a peaceful march in Memphis on behalf of the black garbage collectors. The following day a mule-drawn cart carried the coffin of Martin Luther King Jr. to his final resting place in Atlanta. Fifty thousand people marched behind the cart. Eight days later the city of Memphis came to terms with the black garbage collectors and settled the strike.

The evening before his death, King had addressed some of the striking workers. During his speech he said that, like Moses, he had been to the mountaintop and had seen the promised land. "I might not get there with you. But I want you to know tonight that we as a people will get to the Promised Land. . . . I'm not worried about anything. I'm not fearing any man. Mine eyes have seen the glory of the coming of the Lord." [18]

Soldiers patrol the streets in the aftermath of riots that erupted following the assassination of Martin Luther King Jr.

A mule-drawn cart carries the casket of Dr. Martin Luther King Jr. from Ebenezer Church en route to his final resting place.

The words he spoke are a testament to the courage of a man who believed that ordinary people acting together could move the most difficult obstacles and that right would ultimately win. "I believe that unarmed truth and unconditional love will have the final word in reality. That is why right, temporarily defeated, is stronger than evil triumphant." [19] Martin Luther King Jr.'s life was proof of that statement.

CHAPTER 5

Malcolm X: A Voice of Anger

One evening in April 1957, a crowd of some two thousand people gathered outside a police station in the part of New York City

Unlike Dr. Martin Luther King Jr., Malcolm X believed that equality for blacks should be achieved by any means necessary, including violence.

known as Harlem. They had assembled out of concern for a man who had been beaten and arrested by the police. A young black man named Malcolm X arrived and went into the station to check on the condition of the man, who was known as Brother Hinton. Malcolm protested the lack of medical care and made the police agree to send Hinton to a local hospital to have his wounds treated. In exchange for that, the nervous police officers asked Malcolm to make the assembled crowd go home. Malcolm X walked outside. With a simple wave of his hand, the crowd dispersed. Both the police and some other members of the Harlem community wondered who this young man was.

An Early Acquaintance with Hate

The man known to the public as Malcolm X was born Malcolm Little on May 9, 1925, in Omaha, Nebraska. His father was Reverend Earl Little, an outspoken man who used his pulpit to preach to his parishioners that they should take pride in their race and culture. Malcom's mother, Louise, was a fair-skinned woman from the island of Grenada in the Caribbean.

Reverend Little's outspokenness upset some whites in Omaha. One night a band of thugs came to terrorize his family and threaten to destroy their home. Earl Little moved the family to Lansing, Michigan, but four years later, in 1929, their home was destroyed by fire, possibly by a group of whites angered by Little's message of black pride and self-reliance. Earl Little refused to be intimidated, which may well have led to his death. One night Little's body was found lying across a streetcar track. His skull was smashed and his body cut almost in two. Little's family suspected he had been killed by whites who feared his potential for stirring up trouble in the black community.

Without Earl Little's support, the family faced financial troubles. The whole country was in the midst of the Great Depression, and many families had to seek help from the government. Louise Little had to accept welfare in order to keep her family alive. The strain was too great for her, though. Malcolm's mother suffered such emotional distress that she was sent to a mental hospital in Kalamazoo, Michigan. Her children were separated and sent to live with other families in the Lansing area.

Malcolm alternately did well in school and got into trouble. Since not many blacks lived in the Lansing area, he was often the only black student in his class. He got along well with his classmates, although he eventually realized that they thought of him not as their equal but as a kind of mascot.

Malcolm X's grade school, Pleasant Grove, in Lansing, Michigan.

Malcolm found that his teachers had their own ideas of what a black student could accomplish. For example, a white teacher whom Malcolm had admired discouraged him from becoming a lawyer, saying it was an unrealistic goal for a black person. Insulted and hurt, Malcolm decided that he wanted to live someplace where more blacks lived and his talents would be appreciated. His half sister Ella lived in Boston, and Malcolm went to live with her.

A New World

Boston was a completely new world for Malcolm. Ella lived in a well-to-do black neighborhood known as Sugar Hill. Malcolm, however, felt more at home in the rougher Roxbury area, where it seemed to him that blacks were more themselves and less concerned with imitating the white middle class.

In Roxbury, Malcolm enjoyed "hanging out" in local pool halls. In one of the pool halls, Malcolm met a boy named "Shorty," who worked racking balls. With Shorty's help, Malcolm got a job shining shoes. Some of Malcolm's customers were hustlers, men who are always on the lookout for ways to take advantage of every situation. From these customers, Malcolm learned to be a hustler himself, and he quickly became involved in the gambling, the illegal liquor trade, and the prostitution that thrived around the pool halls and nightclubs of Roxbury.

On the streets of Boston, Malcolm X became a hustler and devoted his intelligence to making money in gambling, bootleg liquor, and prostitution.

Following the lead of some of the men he met, Malcolm wanted to look more like a white man. Part of that effort involved straightening his hair by using harsh chemicals. In another effort to be stylish, he bought a zoot suit. Such suits were popular among men of the time, and they featured big ballooning trousers and a coat with tails that reached the knees. Wearing his suit and sporting his straightened hair, Malcolm felt like a cool cat.

On to New York

Malcolm needed money to support his new image. He moved from shining shoes to a job working on the railroad as a cook in the dining car. The train Malcolm worked on ran between Boston and New York City. Most nights he partied in New York, sleeping just a few hours before reporting for the return trip to Boston. When he was in Boston, he spent his spare time with Shorty and with his own girlfriend, a white girl named Sophia. He smoked marijuana, drank, and experimented with other drugs. Naturally, this activity interfered with his work, and he got fired from a variety of railroad jobs. Finally, he ended up living in Harlem, where he worked as a waiter at a nightclub called Small's Paradise.

Small's Paradise was a popular hangout for many of Harlem's criminals. Malcolm knew that Charlie Small, the owner of the nightclub, wanted no trouble from the police and forbade any of his employees from engaging in criminal acts, but Malcolm decided to offer to find a prostitute for a man who looked like a lonely soldier. That man was really an undercover policeman who promptly took Malcolm into custody. Malcolm did not have a police record, so he was let go with a warning. Charlie Small, however, was not so forgiving. He fired Malcolm and told him never to enter the club again.

Without a job, Malcolm turned for help to a man named Sammy, who suggested that Malcolm could make some money selling marijuana. Malcolm was soon making a handsome profit. He became involved in selling other illegal drugs, such as heroin. In addition, he engaged in "steering" wealthy, important men to prostitutes in Harlem.

Trouble in Boston

In the course of his activities, Malcolm became an enemy of some dangerous people, including a man known as West Indian Archie. Malcolm's life was threatened, and he made a hasty return to Boston, where he and his friend Shorty joined up with Malcolm's old girlfriend, Sophia. To bring in money, they started a burglary ring. Sophia and her sister would find work as maids for wealthy families. As they worked, they would note the location of the family's valuables. Malcolm and his partners would break in during the night to steal the items that Sophia and her sister had identified. The scheme worked well until Malcolm made a mistake.

Malcolm took one of the stolen items, a beautiful antique watch, into a repair shop. All the repair shops had been told by police to be on the lookout for this distinctive watch. Malcolm and the rest of the gang were soon arrested. At his trial, Malcolm was found guilty and was sentenced to five to ten years in prison.

In Prison

At twenty-one years of age, Malcolm Little found himself in Charlestown State Prison. Malcolm refused to follow prison rules, and his surly attitude toward the prison guards often earned him a stay in solitary confinement. He cursed everyone in sight and God as well. It was his cursing of God that earned him the nickname "Satan."

After a while, however, another prisoner, a black man named Bimbi, began to have an influence on Malcolm. Bimbi was a soft-spoken man who commanded total respect from the other prisoners, and that impressed Malcolm. Bimbi recognized that Malcolm was smart, and he advised him to use his intelligence to get an education.

Malcolm followed that advice. Although privately he saw his efforts as just a way to manipulate the prison system to gain privileges, he studied English, learned Latin, and took other college courses by mail. Education, which had started for Malcolm as a way to get privileges in prison, became something he valued. Years later he would say, "Without an education, you're not going anywhere in this world." [20]

Malcolm's behavior improved as well. With help from his half sister Ella, he was able to transfer to an experimental prison, the Norfolk Prison Colony. There, he found an extensive library that he used to learn about world history and religions.

A New Faith

It was at Norfolk that Malcolm first became interested in the teachings of a man known as Elijah Muhammed, who called himself "the Messenger of Allah." Mr. Muhammed, as his followers called him, preached that the true religion of blacks was Islam because that had been the religion of many West Africans before they were captured and brought to America as slaves. Mr. Muhammed's teachings, however, focused on whites as evil beings. Blacks, he said, should reject the white man's ways and return to the state of dignity and honor they had known in Africa. They were to cleanse themselves completely of the white man's world and become totally self-sufficient and separate from whites. Black Muslims, as Muhammed's followers were known, obeyed strict rules against drinking, smoking, taking drugs, or dancing. They could not eat pork or engage in activities like gambling, going to movies, dancing, dating, or having sex outside of marriage.

Elijah Muhammed, leader of the Black Muslims and an important influence on Malcolm X, preaches to his congregation.

Malcolm's brothers Philbert and Reginald had already become Black Muslims. Malcolm listened to the ideas they shared with him. He began to read every book he could obtain on Islam, black civilizations in Africa, slavery, and the history of blacks in America. He even began to write directly to Elijah Muhammed. By the time Malcolm was paroled in 1953, he had become a different man from the one who had been locked up seven years earlier. He left prison determined to live his life according to the teachings of Elijah Muhammed; it was a decision that would change his life permanently.

Upon his release, Malcolm moved to Detroit to live with his brother Wilfred, who had also become a member of the Black Muslims. Malcolm attended services at Detroit Temple Number One. It was there that Malcolm first met Elijah Muhammed in person. Mr. Muhammed was soft-spoken and gentle in appearance, but, as he addressed the people in the temple, his words fired Malcolm's imagination. To Malcolm's surprise, Elijah Muhammed called his name and told the gathering about this young man

Malcolm X's brothers in 1949. It was their adoption of Islam that led Malcolm to join the Black Muslims.

who had been writing him from prison. He said that he believed that Malcolm had truly given up the devil and would remain faithful to his new religion.

From Malcolm Little to Malcolm X

Later that evening at a dinner held at Elijah Muhammed's home, Malcolm formally accepted Islam. As a member of the Nation of Islam, his surname was replaced by an X. The X stood for the ancestral African family name that blacks had lost when they were enslaved.

Malcolm X thrived in his new community and became active in recruiting new members to the Nation of Islam. In late 1953 Elijah Muhammed sent Malcolm back to Boston to recruit in the black community there. He succeeded in setting up a temple in Boston and, shortly after, one in Philadelphia. Then came the biggest challenge: Elijah Muhammed sent Malcolm to Harlem, home of some 1 million black people. Mr. Muhammed reasoned that if the Black Muslims were to become a major force in the lives of blacks, such a large black community had to have a temple of its own.

Malcolm X returned to New York looking quite different from the way he had in the old days. He was dressed in a plain suit, white shirt, and a tie. His hair was no longer straightened, and he now wore glasses. His keen intelligence remained unchanged, however, and he set to work attracting new members to the Nation of Islam. He printed flyers with information about the Nation of Islam and handed them out to passersby. He spoke on street corners about the evil that whites had done to blacks and about how Christianity was used by whites to keep blacks from making demands for justice. Malcolm's persistent efforts paid off, and gradually Temple Number Seven grew.

Media Attention

In 1959, with the airing by CBS Television of the documentary "The Hate That Hate Produced," media interest focused on the Muslims and Malcolm X, who became the informal spokesperson for the Nation of Islam. He appeared on radio and on television, and he was invited to speak on university campuses. Malcolm proved equal to the challenge. His sharp mind and even sharper tongue surprised and frightened many Americans both white and black. For instance, when asked whether he preached hate, he gave this rapid-fire answer:

Malcolm X became a passionate and articulate speaker who captured the attention of the nation with his fiery oratory.

How can anybody ask us do we hate the white man who kidnapped us four hundred years ago, brought us here and stripped us of our history, stripped us of our culture, stripped us of our language, stripped us of everything you could have used today to prove that you're a part of the human family, bring you down to the level of an animal, sell you from plantation to plantation like a sack of wheat, sell you like a sack of potatos, sell you like a horse and a plow, and then hung you up from one end of the country to the other, and then you ask me do I hate him? Why, your question is worthless! [21]

An Angry Voice

Malcolm became the angry voice that expressed the pent-up frustrations of many black people. As a result of Malcolm X's efforts, membership in the Nation of Islam began to grow. By 1960 Muslim temples existed in most major American cities, and in 1961 plans to build a $20-million Islamic center in Chicago were unveiled.

Meanwhile, Malcolm X had met and fallen in love with Sister Betty X, who taught nursing to other Muslim women in Harlem. Although Betty's upper-class family did not approve, Betty married Malcolm in January 1958. They began a family soon after and settled down in a quiet neighborhood in Queens in a home provided by the Nation of Islam.

As the 1960s opened, the events of the civil rights movement caught the nation's attention. Demonstrations held in the South to achieve integration of public facilities often resulted in the black participants' being insulted, abused, and arrested by white authorities. Elijah Muhammed and the Black Muslims did not favor integration and saw no role for themselves in the confrontations happening in the South.

Meanwhile on the streets of Harlem, people commented on how the Muslims talked tough but never took any direct action. To many blacks, it seemed that it was the followers of Martin Luther King Jr. who were fighting and winning the battles. Malcolm had to be content to sit on the sidelines and mock the demonstrators for just "getting their heads whipped." [22] Malcolm X was frustrated by the Nation of Islam's lack of action, but he could do nothing about it.

Troubles in the Nation of Islam

As his frustration grew, Malcolm X began to find himself at odds with fellow Muslims. When Elijah Muhammed had left Chicago to live in Arizona for health reasons, for example, rumors began to circulate that Malcolm was taking credit for developing the Black Muslim organization and was making lots of money doing it. Malcolm, in fact, had only accepted enough money for his family to live on and to cover his travel expenses. Despite the rumors, Malcolm still had Mr. Muhammed's confidence, and in 1963 he was even named as the first national minister for the Nation of Islam.

Malcolm X's first direct confrontation with Elijah Muhammed came on November 22, 1963, when President John F. Kennedy was assassinated. Elijah Muhammed issued orders that Muslims were to make no comment. However, when Malcolm was asked for his reaction to the president's assassination, he replied, "It's a case of chickens coming home to roost. Being an old farm boy myself, chickens coming home to roost never did make me sad; they've always made me glad." [23] The press interpreted that statement to mean that Malcolm felt that Kennedy had gotten what he deserved. In response to this disobedience, Elijah Muhammed "silenced" Malcolm, issuing an order that Malcolm could not speak for the Muslim organization, teach in the temples, or address audiences of the Muslim faithful for ninety days. Malcolm used this time to think about his situation and decide his future moves.

After the ninety days had passed, Malcolm X called a press conference. During the conference he stated that, although he was still a Muslim and believed in Mr. Muhammed's teachings, there were other goals that needed to be accomplished, such as obtaining good jobs, housing, and education for black people. He called on other black leaders to join him in his ef-

Malcolm X's comments to the press after the Kennedy assassination put him at odds with Elijah Muhammed and the rest of the Black Muslims.

forts. He also announced that he would set up his own temple, Muslim Mosque, Inc., in New York to provide a place for all black people, regardless of their religion, to actively participate in social and economic programs in their community. In response to Malcolm's announcement, the Black Muslims demanded that he and his family leave the house in Queens. Malcolm X knew that other black leaders mistrusted him and that the Black Muslim organization was now soundly against him. Amid all this activity, Malcolm X prepared to embark on a journey that would radically change his life. He needed to consider his future, and he decided to take a trip that he had long dreamed of: a holy pilgrimage to the city of Mecca.

A Holy Pilgrimage

In April 1964 Malcolm X quietly left the United States. The flight to Mecca was an eye-opening experience; he was amazed

After a ninety-day silence, Malcolm X held a brief press conference following which he left the country for a pilgrimage to the holy city of Mecca.

by the wide variety of people he saw who were also Muslims. They came from all over the world and were of every race.

Malcolm stopped in Jidda, located just forty miles from Mecca. Mecca is Islam's holiest city, and non-Muslims are not allowed inside its walls, so Malcolm had to appear before a special court that would decide if he were truly a Muslim before allowing him to enter Mecca. Malcolm presented an especially unusual case because there were so few Muslims from the United States. Finally, with the help of Omar Azzam, a member of the Saudi royal family whose telephone number Malcolm had been given before he left the United States, Malcolm was permitted to enter Mecca.

Once in Mecca, Malcolm completed the rituals of worship in which all Muslim pilgrims must participate. As he saw people of all different backgrounds and races living and worshiping together, Malcolm X's thinking on race began to change. Upon completing the pilgrimage, Malcolm assumed the Muslim name el Hajj Malik el Shabazz. More than just his name was altered, however; he came away from the experience a different person.

A New Malcolm

Malcolm's journey left him with a clearer purpose. Upon his return to the United States, he announced the creation of the Organization of Afro-American Unity (OAAU). In his announcement, Malcolm stated his willingness to work with any person who wanted to improve the human condition. He tried to show that he was not so far apart from Martin Luther King Jr. by saying, "Dr. King wants the same thing I do—freedom!"[24] Malcolm's new attitude may best be captured by a quote in Patricia Robinson's essay "Malcolm X: Our Revolutionary Son and Brother":

Following his pilgrimage, Malcolm X's ideas about race began to change and he tried to moderate the tone of his public comments.

I feel like a man who has been asleep somewhat and under someone else's control. I feel that what I am thinking and saying is now for myself. Before it was for and by the guidance of Elijah Muhammed. Now I think with my own mind.[25]

His more moderate attitude, however, did not get much publicity. Newspapers preferred to print anything he said that sounded like the old threatening Malcolm.

Meanwhile, his relationship with the Nation of Islam had become extremely hostile. The Nation of Islam was still trying to evict his family from the house in Queens. Likewise, its representatives threatened Malcolm's life, and several attempts were made to kill him. Finally, one night in February 1965, his family's home was firebombed. Malcolm was reliving the terror of his childhood, but now he, and not his father, was the target of the assaults.

He rescued his three daughters and his pregnant wife and sent them to live with friends. He was a hunted man, but that did not stop him from rallying a group of followers to develop a new organization to counter the Nation of Islam. This would be a test of his belief that, "if you are not ready to die for it, put the word

Charred furniture sits in front of Malcolm X's house in Queens, New York, after the residence was firebombed.

Malcolm X is comforted by his followers as he lies mortally wounded on a stage in Harlem's Audubon Ballroom on February 21, 1965.

'freedom' out of your head." [26] Malcolm's statement would be put to the test by his own black brothers in the Nation of Islam.

Dying for Freedom

Sunday, February 21, 1965, amid all of the death threats, Malcolm came to the Audubon Ballroom in Harlem to address his followers. Fearing that it would make people afraid to attend the rally, he did not have guards search those who entered. As he began his address, a loud argument broke out in the middle of the hall. Malcolm's bodyguards ran to break up the fight, and at that moment, three men stood up directly in front of the stage where Malcolm was standing and shot him. He was hit multiple times in the chest and fell over backwards. Before ambulance crews could arrive on the scene, Malcolm X was dead.

According to Islamic custom, his body was wrapped in seven layers of white cloth. For six days he lay in state at a funeral home where thousands of Harlem residents filed past to pay their last respects. Although the three Black Muslim men who did the shooting were arrested and later convicted of murder, there is still speculation about the involvement of others in the assassination. What is certain is that a powerful, intelligent leader was lost at just the moment when he was reaching for a way to benefit all people.

CHAPTER 6

Fannie Lou Hamer: An Everyday Heroine

Fanny Lou Hamer was an ordinary woman of extraordinary determination. When asked once by a *New York Times* reporter why she stayed in Mississippi, she replied,

> Why should I leave Ruleville, and why should I leave Mississippi? I go to the big city with the kind of education they give us here in Mississippi, I got problems. . . . That's why I want to change things in Mississippi. You don't run away from problems—you just face them.[27]

Hamer's life is a testament to that belief.

On October 6, 1917, Fannie Lou Townsend was born into a family of Mississippi sharecroppers, the twentieth child of Jim and Lou Ella Townsend. Everyone had to work if the family was to survive, so at the age of six, Fannie Lou began working in the cotton fields. She later remembered that the plantation's owner had offered to buy her some candy if she could pick thirty pounds of cotton that day. She picked her thirty pounds, proving to the owner that she was ready for work. By the next week she was picking sixty pounds of cotton a day and receiving no special treats for doing it.

A Precarious Prosperity

Sometimes a sharecropper and his family could earn and save enough money to begin to get ahead. All of the Townsends worked in the fields, and by the time Fannie Lou was twelve, her family had been able to rent a few acres and an old house for their own use. They even had managed to buy a few farm animals.

The Townsends were prospering in a small way, something that local whites could not tolerate. One night someone put an insecticide called Paris green into the Townsends' animal feed. The poison killed the mules the family relied on to plow their fields and the cow that provided them with milk. Without these essential animals, the Townsends were forced to go back to being sharecroppers.

The Townsends knew that education was the key to a better life, so Fannie Lou had been attending school. Even though the school year was only four months long, so as not to interfere with the labor supply for the cotton growers, Fannie Lou learned to read and write. After her family returned to sharecropping, though, she had to quit school so that she could devote all of her time to helping in the fields. Although her formal education ended in the sixth grade, she developed her reading skills further by reading the Bible regularly with other members of the Stranger's Home Baptist Church.

The hard life that the Townsend family led became harder with the coming of the Great Depression. The low price brought by the cotton they grew meant that their share of the crop did not bring enough money to support the family. Once the family had finished with the harvest on the land they sharecropped, they would go from plantation to plantation to pick any leftover cotton from the fields, which they would sell. Fannie Lou would also help local farmers slaughter hogs. As payment, she

Fannie Lou Hamer crusaded to improve the lives of blacks in rural Mississippi.

would be given the intestines, the feet, and the head. These leftovers were used to supplement the family's diet, but sometimes the only food the Townsends had to eat was bread and onions.

Adding to the family's troubles, the elder Townsends' health began to fail. Jim Townsend had a stroke in 1939, and Fannie Lou's mother slowly began going blind after an accident she suffered while helping to clear timber. In the face of these misfortunes, Lou Ella remained proud and taught Fannie Lou to always respect herself. Fannie Lou did not know what to do about all that she saw and experienced, but she prayed to God to give her a chance to do something about the conditions she lived under in Mississippi.

Signs of Change

Change, however slight, was on the way. During the years of World War II, life began to improve for the blacks in the United

States. The war created a need for workers in the factories that made war supplies. When President Franklin D. Roosevelt signed Executive Order 8802, banning racial discrimination in hiring in government and in the defense industries, many blacks got their first jobs besides farming. These new workers received paychecks for the first time, and though the salaries were low, blacks began to expect a better life.

President Franklin D. Roosevelt's Executive Order 8802 banned discrimination in the defense industry.

In addition, black soldiers who were fighting overseas, though still in a segregated military, began demanding treatment equal to that given white soldiers. New civil rights organizations like the Congress of Racial Equality (CORE) were founded to support the fight against fascism overseas and to end racism in the United States.

In the cotton fields of Mississippi, Fannie Lou heard little of these events in the outside world. In 1944, at the age of twenty-seven, she married a farmworker named Perry "Pap" Hamer and settled down to work in the fields as her mother and grandmother had done before her. Sometimes she cleaned houses of white people to make extra money.

Hamer and her husband set out to make a life for themselves. When they realized that Fannie Lou was unable to bear children, they adopted two daughters, Dorothy Jean and Virgie Lee. Though Hamer hoped their lives would be better than hers, she still did not know what one woman could do to make a real difference. Yet she was destined to make that difference.

By 1962 Fannie Lou Hamer was forty-four years old and had worked for thirty-eight years in the cotton fields. Though she was aware of the events of the 1950s in which blacks had successfully protested their unequal treatment elsewhere in the South, her life in Ruleville, Mississippi, continued as it always had.

A New Life

On Sunday, August 26, 1962, however, something did happen that would make a difference in Hamer's life. The minister at her church announced a mass meeting to be held the next evening. It would be cosponsored by the Student Nonviolent Coordinating Committee (SNCC) and the Southern Christian Leadership Conference (SCLC), and it would be held at the church. No one knew exactly what to expect, but the fact that the meeting was to be held at the church meant that it would be important.

James Bevel, the SCLC field secretary for Mississippi, and James Forman, the executive secretary for the SNCC, had come to encourage people to register to vote. Hamer and many of her neighbors did not even know that they had the right to vote, let alone how to go about registering. When the two men asked for volunteers to go to the courthouse to register, Hamer raised her hand. Despite the chance that whites might violently oppose any attempt to register, Hamer and seventeen others vowed to make the attempt.

An Attempt to Vote

The eighteen prospective voters traveled to the county seat, Indianola, in an old yellow bus that was ordinarily used to carry workers to the fields. When they entered the registrar's office, the clerk, Cecil B. Campbell, told them that they had to pass a test in order to register and that only two at a time could take the test. The first part of the test was simple, containing questions about the person's name, address, place of employment, and so on. The second part, however, included detailed questions about the state constitution. Hamer later commented, "I didn't even know Mississippi had a constitution."[28]

It took all day for the eighteen people to take their exams, two at a time, and none of them passed. To add insult to injury, on the way back to Ruleville, the police pulled them over and gave them a one-hundred-dollar ticket because their bus was too close to the shade of yellow used for a school bus. But worse harassment was to come.

When Hamer got home that evening, she learned that the plantation manager, Mr. Marlowe, was angry that she had gone to register to vote. He demanded that she withdraw her registration or leave her home, which was plantation property. That evening Fannie Lou Hamer left her family and moved into the home of some friends who lived in town. Her husband and daughters had to remain on the plantation or else they would lose their jobs as well. It was a nervous time for the Hamers and with good reason.

Just ten days later a group of white men came through town late one night firing shotguns at the home where Hamer was staying and at the homes where a group of SNCC volunteers were staying.

Hamer was unhurt, but two young women students were wounded. Hamer fled to Tallahatchie County, to the home of her niece. For the moment, at least, she was out of danger.

The leaders of the SNCC sensed that in Hamer they had found a potential leader. They sent one of their volunteers, Charles McLaurin, to find Hamer and arrange for her to attend the SNCC's national conference, which was being held in Nashville, Tennessee.

At the conference, Hamer had a chance to learn more about the organization she had joined. The SNCC differed from other civil rights organizations in that it believed in sending volunteers to all of the small, forgotten towns and villages in the South to help the black population organize itself to protest and change the difficult conditions in which they lived. SNCC leaders knew that these "grassroots" efforts to organize the ordinary citizens of these small towns needed to be inspired by someone from the community who could serve as an example of courage. They believed that Fannie Lou Hamer was one such person and appointed her as the SNCC's field secretary for her community.

A Grassroots Activist

Fanny Lou Hamer returned to Ruleville to find that her family had been evicted from the plantation where Pap Hamer had worked for

Fannie Lou Hamer's courage caught the attention of several SNCC volunteers, and she was given the chance to attend SNCC's national conference in Nashville, Tennessee.

thirty years. Still worse, their personal belongings had been confiscated, and no one would hire Pap because he was married to someone who was labeled a troublemaker. A friend found the family a house to live in, although it had no running water.

Amid all of this turmoil, Hamer's first act as an SNCC leader was return to Indianola to try again to register to vote. Determined to succeed, she told the registrar that she would return every month until she passed the test.

In her new role as field secretary for the SNCC, Hamer began organizing a local program to fight poverty by helping poor people receive food and clothing from the federal government. As she helped people obtain these basic necessities, she also tried to convince them to register to vote.

In response to Hamer's activities, the local authorities continued to harass her family. Although the house their friend had found them had no running water, the family received a nine-thousand-dollar water bill from the local water district. When he did not pay this bill, Pap Hamer was arrested. Another time police officers barged into the Hamers' bedroom one morning carrying shotguns as they conducted a search of the premises.

In addition to the harassment, the Hamers suffered extreme poverty because no one would hire any member of the family. They lived on Fannie Lou's ten-dollars-a-week salary from the SNCC, which was supplemented by what their friends could offer in assistance.

A Registered Voter at Last

In spite of the troubles she faced, Hamer continued her efforts to register to vote. On January 10, 1963, she passed the test and registered to vote. This was a victory at the time, but not a complete one. When elections were held in the fall of that year, Hamer was still unable to participate because she could not afford to pay Mississippi's poll tax.

Those who opposed registration of black voters had other more brutal methods available to them as well. In June 1963, after attending an SNCC voter registration workshop in Charleston, South Carolina, Hamer was on her way back to Ruleville when the Continental Trailways bus she and her companions were riding on stopped at the local bus station in Winona, Mississippi. Several of her companions left the bus to get something to eat or to use the rest rooms.

Hamer, who had remained on the bus, saw her companions all come running out of the station. When she got off to find out what was happening, she and six others were taken by the local police to the county jail, although just what they were accused of was never made clear. The county jail was far out in the country. Hamer recalls, "If we could be far enough out, they didn't care how loud we hollered, wasn't nobody gon' hear us."[29] Hamer was kicked and punched, cursed at, and spat on. She was forced to lie face down on a bunk bed, and two black prisoners were ordered to hold her down as white guards took turns using blackjacks to beat her.

Fannie Lou Hamer was in serious trouble, far from anyone who could help her. When the SNCC sent a representative to try to gain the release of the prisoners, he was also arrested and beaten. The police officers offered to free the prisoners at one point, but Hamer and the others were concerned that the police were trying to make it appear that they had tried to escape and could thus justify killing them all. As a result, they chose to remain in jail. Only when Andrew Young and James Bevel, of the SCLC, appealed for help from the U.S. Justice Department were the prisoners released.

Hamer had suffered severe injuries in the beatings, but she needed a Justice Department escort to get medical treatment in Greenwood, Mississippi. She suffered damage to her kidneys and permanent damage to her left eye. From Greenwood she went to Atlanta, Georgia, to recuperate in the home of some civil rights supporters.

Despite the effort she had made and the suffering she had undergone, Fannie Lou Hamer had yet to cast a ballot. However, 1964 started on a hopeful note. On January 23 the states ratified the Twenty-fourth Amendment to the Constitution, which abolished poll taxes. That winter the SNCC and CORE created the Council of Federated Organizations (COFO), which would be involved in grassroots efforts to bring improved education to poor blacks and to register them to vote. COFO conceived a plan to bring hundreds of white volunteers from outside the South into Mississippi that summer to help in their efforts. Having blacks and whites working together, leaders hoped, would draw attention to the effort. The whole nation would be following the events in Mississippi.

A New Democratic Party

That summer organizers descended on Mississippi. With the help of Fannie Lou Hamer and other local leaders, an alternative to Mississippi's old Democratic Party was created. The Mississippi Freedom Democratic Party (MFDP) challenged the authority of the Mississippi Democrats who did not permit blacks to run for office or vote in primary elections.

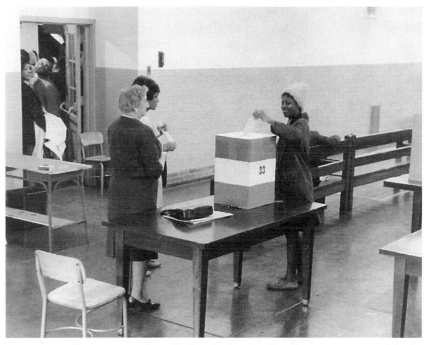

Because poll taxes were legally banned in early 1964, many more blacks were able to cast their votes in the presidential election that year.

Since 1964 was a presidential election year, the MFDP was prepared to attend the Democratic National Convention in Atlantic City, New Jersey, and challenge the Mississippi Democrats for delegate seats at the convention. Hamer would be the vice chair of the delegation.

President Lyndon B. Johnson did not want a battle at the convention between the white Mississippi Democrats and the MFDP, which represented much of the state's large black population. Johnson had just signed the Civil Rights Act of 1964, and he was anxious not to lose his political support in the white South. He decided, therefore, at the beginning of the convention, to block the MFDP efforts to be selected as the state's delegation.

The dispute over who would represent Mississippi would be decided by the Credentials Committee. On August 22 Fannie Lou Hamer testified before the committee. The hearing was televised, and she took the opportunity to question America in general about its treatment of blacks. Her down-to-earth honesty and plain-spoken manner appealed to many Americans, especially her simple statement, "I'm sick and tired of being sick and tired." [30]

Hamer's speech generated a flood of public support for the MFDP, and Johnson realized that he needed to arrange a deal. As

a compromise, the MFDP was offered two seats "at large," meaning that they would not be considered representatives of Mississippi. The proposal disgusted Hamer, and she passionately urged the MFDP to reject the offer saying, "We didn't come all this way for no two seats when all of us is tired." [31] The MFDP felt betrayed, but one effect of the incident was to demonstrate to the nation how southern blacks were being denied their right to vote.

The issue of voters' rights continued to be of great concern for blacks, and in early 1965 President Johnson proposed new voting rights legislation. The resulting Voting Rights Act of 1965 outlawed literacy tests and other practices that had kept African Americans from registering to vote. Fannie Lou Hamer saw that it would now be possible to increase the number of black voters, but she knew that registering blacks to vote was not the whole story.

Fannie Lou Hamer participates in a civil rights march in Hattiesburg, Mississippi.

Running for Office

Hamer realized that even when blacks voted, they often were faced with choosing among politicians who did not speak for them. In response to the need she saw for greater diversity among candidates, she ran for Congress against James Whitten, who followed the party line of the old Democratic Party. Since the all-white Democratic Party did not allow black candidates to appear on the ballot, the SNCC helped the MFDP hold a separate election with Hamer as its candidate. Hamer won this election, so suddenly there were two elected representatives from the same congressional district. Although the MFDP claim to the seat was defeated by a vote in the House of Representatives, the dispute was enough to persuade a federal court to rule the election process in Mississippi illegal. African Americans were determined to make their voices heard, and Fannie Lou Hamer would be one of those voices.

When the next Democratic National Convention was held in 1968, the MFDP, now known as the Mississippi Loyalist Democratic Party (MLDP), enjoyed broader support among sympathetic whites from the regular party. When it came time for delegates to be seated, the MLDP refused to compromise. The old party was forced to integrate. When Hamer took her seat at the convention, she received a standing ovation from the other delegates.

Fannie Lou Hamer became a major voice on behalf of civil rights and eventually ran for office in the Mississippi state senate.

With her membership confirmed, Hamer became an active member of the Democratic Party. From 1968–1971, she served as a member of the Democratic National Committee, the body that directs all of the party's activities. Hamer used her position to influence party policies, representing in particular the point of view of blacks. She did not stop there, entering the field of politics as a candidate for elected office. Hamer ran for a seat in the Mississippi state senate in 1971, and, though she did not win, the fact that a black sharecopper's daughter could run for public office represented a revolution in southern politics.

In her final years, Hamer created a farm cooperative, known as the Freedom Farm, which gave people the opportunity to grow their own food. She was able to help over five thousand people in this way. This tireless voice for improving conditions for blacks was silenced just a few years later. On March 14, 1977, Fannie Lou Hamer died from complications of cancer, high blood pressure, and diabetes. She left a powerful legacy to all those who follow.

CHAPTER 7

Jesse Jackson: Preacher and Politician

Jesse Jackson grew up in Greenville, South Carolina, learning the unwritten rules that both whites and blacks lived by in the South. He learned that when a white person came walking down the sidewalk from the other direction, a black person must step out of the way to let the white person pass. Early on he learned that blacks could spend their money in Greenville's shops, but they could not work in those shops. He also learned to be patient when waiting for service in local stores because white customers always came first. In myriad ways it was made clear that blacks were not to expect treatment equal to that accorded to whites.

From the time he was born, on October 8, 1941, Jesse had to cope with another form of injustice. In the closely knit, devoutly religious black community of Greenville, Jesse's mother, Helen Burns, had borne her son out of wedlock. Though she was a promising music student, the pregnancy forced her to drop out of school and thereby lose several music scholarships that would have allowed her to continue her studies. Just as scandalous was the fact that his father, Noah Robinson, already had a wife and children.

Determined to Be Somebody

Though Jesse was adopted at the age of four by Charles Jackson, the man who eventually married Helen Burns, young Jesse grew up wondering about his own identity. It strengthened his determination to be somebody important and to change the world around him. Jackson later wrote, in response to a fifth-grader's question about what Jackson had dreamed about as a little boy, that, "Like many children, I dreamed of good things to come. . . . But at the time when I grew up and I realized that many grownups and many children could not find happiness, I began dreaming of a better world for everyone." [32]

Even as a youngster, Jesse Jackson began to show the leadership abilities that would later serve him so well. In high school he was class president and president of the school's Honor Society. Other students liked him for his good sense of humor and admired his athletic abilities.

Jesse Jackson leads a march across the historic Edmund Pettus Bridge in Selma, Alabama.

Off to Chicago

Being a high school athlete earned Jackson opportunities that most students never receive, but the roots of racial discrimination wove themselves into those opportunities. For example, in 1959 the Chicago White Sox offered Jackson six thousand dollars to play baseball for them. Jackson had thought that it was a good offer until he learned that white recruits were being offered more money. He decided instead to accept a scholarship to play football at the University of Illinois at Chicago.

Jackson spent only a year at the university, but that time opened his eyes to discrimination, northern style. "Up South," as Jackson began to call the North, his skills as a quarterback were completely ignored because blacks were rarely given that leadership position. Black students on campus did not have places where they could get together and socialize, whereas white students could join fraternities and sororities, which did not admit blacks. Jackson remembers that blacks were not even invited to attend a concert by black jazz musician Lionel Hampton that was held at the university. Disappointed with what he found in the North, Jackson returned to the South to finish his college education.

He chose North Carolina Agricultural and Technical State University. Jesse Jackson flourished in North Carolina. He earned the position of quarterback on the university's football team, was elected class president, joined Omega Psi Phi fraternity, and kept up with his studies. He also found time to participate in the growing civil rights movement.

A New Activist and a Call to Preach

Protests at that time, such as sit-ins at local lunch counters, were contributing to a climate of social activism, and Jackson took part in the activities of local civil rights organizations. One of the civil rights groups active on campus was the Congress of Racial Equality (CORE). CORE's leaders recognized Jackson's public speaking ability and put it to use organizing students to participate in the sit-ins and local protest marches.

As he worked for CORE, Jackson observed the important role that black ministers played in motivating people to take action and in organizing their protest effort. Moreover, even as a child Jackson had had the ability to see a grander vision of life. As Jackson biographer Marshall Frady points out, even Jesse's grandmother would say "Jesse can see." [33] Jackson began to think seriously about going into the ministry and talked to Samuel Proctor, the campus chaplain, about becoming a clergyman. Proctor advised Jackson to take his childhood visions seriously as a call to preach.

Jackson did not decide right away on a career, however. He worked for a while for North Carolina's governor at the time, Terry Sanford, organizing clubs for young Democrats. In addition, he continued to closely follow events in the civil rights movement.

Jackson also fell in love. His work with the student protesters had brought him into contact with a fellow student named Jacqueline Brown. Jacqueline recalls being insulted when she passed by a group of football players on campus and heard Jackson call out "Hey girl, I'm going to marry you," but ultimately found herself attracted to "so many things. He's a real warm guy. Real nice. A nice human being."[34] Jackson's prediction came true, and in 1962 they married. Jacqueline was also committed to the struggle for civil rights, and together they continued their participation in civil rights activities.

The bravery and dedication of the leaders of the civil rights movement impressed Jackson, and he made a point of learning more about them. In particular, Martin Luther King Jr.'s "Letter from Birmingham Jail" had a profound effect on Jackson. He felt that King had beautifully captured the essence of what blacks were demanding. He familiarized himself with the efforts of Fannie Lou Hamer to gain voting rights for blacks and power within the Democratic Party. He learned of the contributions of past leaders such as W. E. B. Du Bois and A. Philip Randolph. He also listened to some of the angrier voices, including Malcolm X of the Nation of Islam and Stokely Carmichael and John Lewis of the SNCC.

Jackson felt that his destiny was to play a bigger role in the civil rights movement and that becoming a minister would help him fulfill it. In 1965 he moved to Chicago and enrolled in the Chicago Theological Seminary. Jackson settled his new family, which now included daughter Santita, in Chicago and immersed himself in his studies.

Meanwhile, events in the South were capturing the attention of the whole nation. In March 1965 Martin Luther King Jr. called for a march from Selma, Alabama, to Montgomery to highlight the demand for blacks' voting rights. Jesse Jackson organized a group of other students to drive south to join the march.

Catching King's Eye

Jackson not only participated in the Selma to Montgomery march but also took some leadership initiative himself. He gave a speech

When Jesse Jackson and Jacqueline Brown married in 1962, both found themselves immersed in the fight for civil rights.

to the march participants that, though unauthorized by the march's leadership, nevertheless caught King's attention. Although some people, like longtime King associate Andrew Young, viewed Jackson as an upstart, his self-assured manner impressed King. King also noted that Jackson did not shirk any assigned task, even if the job meant just serving coffee. Once the march was completed, Jackson returned to Chicago and his studies, but King remembered him.

A year later Jackson got the opportunity to work directly with King when King came to Chicago in 1966. Jackson prepared the way for King's arrival. By that time, Jackson was a youth minister at Chicago's Friendship Baptist Church. At Jackson's urging,

Friendship Baptist's leaders aided in securing the help and partic-ipation of Chicago's black churches in organizing the rallies that King was planning.

Meeting King and his family when they arrived in Chicago af-forded Jackson his first taste of dealing with the national press. King gave the young minister some pointers on how to talk to re-porters, though there is some indication that Jackson had a way with members of the press in his own right. As Jackson biographer Marshall Frady remembers, "[Jackson] was a young acolyte of Martin Luther King back around 1966–1967. He seemed then to more journalists than myself to have some special glamour of por-tent about him, some extra electricity." [35]

Jackson organized a huge rally, held in Soldier Field, and then walked with King in a march from Soldier Field to city hall to protest the living conditions for blacks in Chicago's slums. The events convinced Chicago mayor Richard Daley to meet with King and promise to improve conditions in Chicago's public housing projects.

In the end, however, Daley took no action. Though many blacks in Chicago felt that the protest had been pointless, Jackson believed that King's visit had exposed the conditions that poor

Jesse Jackson and Martin Luther King Jr. discussed the economic goals for Chicago's black community with corporate officials.

blacks were experiencing in the North. Now Americans were aware that poverty, malnutrition, and inadequate housing were problems blacks faced nationwide. He also learned from his time with King that it would take sustained effort to change conditions.

Operation Breadbasket

By 1966 King had begun to focus on economic issues in the effort to change living conditions for blacks. Jackson's organizational abilities made him a natural choice to head such an effort. Before he left Chicago, King appointed Jackson director of the Chicago branch of Operation Breadbasket. Operation Breadbasket's goal was to create jobs and to focus black purchasing power as a way of bringing about change. Jackson laid out a campaign that urged blacks to buy products from black-owned companies and to shop at black-owned stores. White-owned stores in black neighborhoods were urged to carry goods made by blacks and to hire more black employees.

Jackson knew that an economic boycott would be needed to force these changes. He also realized that such an effort would work best if it were aimed at a specific target. After careful study of the city's businesses, Jackson called for a boycott of Country Delight, a chain of dairy stores in Chicago. Since dairy products spoil quickly, the boycott was effective, and the company quickly gave in to the demands that it hire some black workers. The next targets were the Red Rooster, a chain of supermarkets in the black community, and A & P Groceries. Both chains were accused of overpricing their goods. As a result of the pressure, A & P changed its hiring and pricing policies. Red Rooster, which also was accused of selling rotten meat to customers in black neighborhoods, refused to change its policies and was driven out of business by the boycott.

Operation Breadbasket demonstrated black purchasing power in other ways. When organizers called for "Black Christmas" and "Black Easter," blacks boycotted the downtown stores during these holiday shopping periods to support their demand that blacks be hired in the stores where they often shopped. Operation Breadbasket also drew public attention to how city funds were invested and pressured the city to support black-owned banks by investing city funds in them.

Operation Breadbasket meetings became one of the black community's major gathering places. Given frequent opportunities to address audiences, Jackson further honed his public speaking skills. To increase attendance at rallies he organized, he arranged for live bands and gospel music. Jackson also used the events to expose those who attended to the thoughts of great African American thinkers and writers such as W. E. B. Du Bois and Langston Hughes. More and more, Jackson was becoming a key player in the civil rights movement. His prominence would soon make him a witness to tragedy.

In late March 1968, as Martin Luther King Jr. planned the Poor People's Campaign, Jackson accompanied King to Memphis to help him in his support of the striking garbage collectors. In the early evening of April 4, 1968, Jackson was preparing to drive King to a restaurant to have dinner. King stepped out onto the balcony of his motel room just above where Jackson was standing. A sniper's bullet struck King in the head, killing him almost instantly.

Disillusioned with what he saw as a lack of leadership within the SCLC, Jackson announced his resignation from the group in 1971.

King's death left a vacuum in the leadership of the civil rights movement. Though many hoped a new black leader would step into King's shoes, no leader with King's stature emerged. In the absence of strong leadership, factions within the SCLC were vying for power. Distressed by the strife between different groups within the SCLC, Jackson resigned from Operation Breadbasket and left the SCLC in 1971.

Pushing Forward

Not satisfied to sit on the sidelines and watch, however, Jackson immediately rallied the Chicago community around a new organization that he formed called People United to Serve Humanity (PUSH). Like Operation Breadbasket, PUSH focused on improving economic conditions for blacks, but the group's main goal was to convince major corporations to focus on blacks in product development, advertising, and hiring.

Jackson's interests, however, did not just focus on the needs of adults. He began to focus on the needs of young black people who were dealing with gangs, drugs, and a lack of self-respect. Wanting to challenge them to improve themselves in all ways, he launched a new movement for black school children known as EXCEL. EXCEL was short for *excellence*, and it focused on practical steps, such as parent-teacher conferences, more parental involvement in student homework, and school attendance, as ways to help young people succeed. EXCEL attracted attention from the national news media, earning it a report on the CBS news program *60 Minutes* in 1977. The federal government noticed too: The U.S. Department of Education gave Jackson a grant to take EXCEL into other schools across the nation.

As Jackson focused on more complex organizing efforts such as EXCEL, he modified his personal style. Gone were the casual clothes, about which King had sometimes teased him. Gone as well were the big Afro hairstyle and the brightly colored African dashikis that he had worn. Jackson trimmed his hair short and wore business suits.

Expanding Horizons

As Jackson worked to expand his influence nationally, he also worked to develop his knowledge of the wider world by traveling to Liberia, Nigeria, South Africa, and the Middle East. In Europe, he toured U.S. military bases, speaking to servicemen and -women.

When he returned from his travels, he decided that he would go into politics, seeing in such a move the possibility of participating in the decision-making process that affected people's daily lives. In 1972, he ran against incumbent mayor Richard Daley for the mayorship of Chicago. He did not expect to win, but he wanted to show that a black person could run for office and appeal to a diverse group of voters.

Jesse Jackson became a powerful voice for minorities and later ran for the Democratic Party's nomination for president of the United States.

In 1983 Jackson made a much larger move into politics when he decided to run for the Democratic Party's nomination for president. He appealed to a diverse group of voters, including blacks, Asians, poor whites, women, Hispanics, and Native Americans, to form what he called the Rainbow Coalition.

A Controversial Campaign

Jackson created controversy during his campaign. For example, Jackson's use of an ethnic slur against Jews (he called New York City "Hymietown"), strained his relationship with Jewish supporters as well as with many other whites and blacks. He apologized, addressing his mistake in a speech given at the Democratic National Convention:

> If in my low moments, in word, deed or attitude, through some error of temper, or tone, I have caused discomfort, created pain or revived someone's fears, that was not my truest self. If there were occasions when my grape turned to a raisin and my joy bell lost its resonance, please forgive me.[36]

Jackson's campaign caught the attention of many Americans, and, although he did not win the party's nomination in 1984, his campaign set the stage for a second, stronger run for the nomination in 1988.

Running Again

Jesse Jackson arrived at the 1988 Democratic National Convention with twelve hundred delegates pledged to vote for him. Massachusetts governor Michael Dukakis won the nomination, but much excitement surrounded Jackson as well. In his speech to the assembled delegates, carried live by all of the commercial television networks, Jackson called America a patchwork quilt of the type his mother used to make: "She took pieces of old cloth . . . only patches . . . but they didn't stay that way long. With sturdy hands and a strong cord, she sewed them together in a quilt, a thing of power, beauty, and culture." [37] Jackson's presence made it clear that black participation in politics had come a long way from the days just fourteen years before when blacks had not even been able to be seated as party delegates.

New Challenges, New Directions

Throughout the 1990s Jackson remained a force within the Democratic Party. He gave a rousing speech at the Democrats' national convention in 1992, in which he used the slogan Keep Hope Alive! In his speech, Jackson stated,

> Some of us are born short, short on hope, short on opportunities . . . but somebody has to measure their giantness by not reaching up but by reaching out and caring and sharing. Democrats, if we pursue that ethic, that love

Presidential candidate Jesse Jackson gives the thumbs up after a speech to senior citizens on Long Island, New York, in 1988.

ethic, that care ethic, we will win, and we will deserve to win. Keep hope alive. Never surrender. Keep hope alive.[38]

Jackson created his own politically oriented television talk show in the early 1990s called *The Jesse Jackson Show*, which was taped before a live audience. Jackson currently has a program on CNN called *Both Sides* in which guests, who represent the opposite sides of a question, explain and debate their views.

Jackson is a person who believes in making dreams come true and offers these words of inspiration: "We've removed the ceiling above our dreams. There are no more impossible dreams." [39] As America moves toward the twenty-first century, Jesse Jackson continues to truly fulfill his claim, "I am somebody!"

CHAPTER 8

Myrlie Evers-Williams: A New Kind of Leader

Dear Danny,

When you were four days old . . . you looked so much like Medgar . . . I picked you up and held you and began to sob. . . . I wondered what you might have to face, a male, African-American child, in this country, in this time. . . . When your grandfather was killed, I was consumed with hatred to the point that my motivation for staying alive was to get even. . . . I simply wanted to take a gun and mow them all down. . . . It brought back something that Medgar said to me not long before he was killed: "Myrlie, hatred of another human being is below you. It destroys you." So I decided to turn my hatred into the more positive force of persistence, to move on in my own life and do what I could do to keep Medgar's memory alive. . . .

I want you to know that your grandfather would be very proud of you for finishing high school, for accomplishing something positive. . . . There are very difficult challenges yet before you . . . but no matter what happens, I don't want you to ever fall into a mode of self-pity and give up on your dreams. . . . Stand with your arms open to all that life has to bring you, whether it is negative or positive, because in doing so, you will become stronger, and your journey through this planet will have real meaning.

Love,
Grandma-ma Myrlie[40]

This passage comes from a letter that Myrlie Evers-Williams wrote to her grandson Danny on the occasion of his high school graduation. The advice she offers comes from the wisdom gained from a lifetime dedicated to fighting for black civil rights. That fight has taken her down a road with many twists and turns, but, as she advises her grandson, she opened her arms to what life had to bring and that, in turn, allowed her to make many valuable contributions to the civil rights movement.

Myrlie Louise Beasley was born in Vicksburg, Mississippi, on March 17, 1933. Her parents divorced when she was an infant and left Myrlie to grow up in the care of her grandmother, Annie McCain Beasley, and her aunt, Myrlie Beasley Polk. These two women were both teachers and placed a high value on education. As an educator, Myrlie's grandmother had a way of making difficult concepts understandable to a young child. She explained the struggles of life in this way:

> God is like the potter. You are the clay. The potter molds the clay into the vessel he wishes it to be, and it can be very beautiful. But that pottery does not become strong, almost unbreakable, until it is placed in the fire. Only then does the real beauty, the real strength shine through.[41]

Annie McCain Beasley's mention of "the fire" was a good way to refer to what blacks had to suffer in the South, especially when they spoke out for their rights. It was not uncommon for white supremacist groups like the Ku Klux Klan to threaten, beat, or murder outspoken blacks in order to intimidate the rest of the black community and prevent further protest against the conditions they faced.

Myrlie's childhood was, by her own description, a sheltered one, although she still had to deal with the racism in the world outside of her home. For example, after graduating from high school she was not able to attend any of the local colleges, which were reserved for white students. To get a college education, she had to go off to Lorman, Mississippi, to attend Alcorn A & M College. In 1950 she enrolled there intending to study education and music.

Civil Rights and Medgar Evers

On the first day of school at Alcorn, Myrlie met a young man majoring in business administration named Medgar Evers. Evers was also a member of the debate team, college choir, business club, football and track teams, and he was the editor of the campus newspaper and yearbook. His kindness and sense of responsibility attracted Myrlie, and she and Medgar Evers were soon dating.

Their relationship deepened, and, on Christmas Eve 1951, a year and a half after their first meeting, Medgar Evers and Myrlie Beasley were married. When Medgar finished his degree in the next spring, the couple moved to the town of Mound Bayou in the Mississippi Delta, where Medgar took a job selling insurance. Myrlie's own plans to finish college were put on hold.

Nothing had prepared the young couple for the poverty and racism that black sharecroppers in the Delta endured. Sharecroppers lived in substandard housing on the cotton plantations where they worked, and there was little someone in such a situation could do to improve his or her circumstances. If he or she disagreed with the owner's policies or did anything that displeased local whites,

When Medgar Evers married Myrlie Beasley in 1951, they were both blind to the many tribulations they would face as a result of their efforts on behalf of black civil rights.

such as trying to register to vote, he or she was subject to eviction as well as possible physical harassment. Out of a desire to improve the situation he had found, Medgar became active in the National Association for the Advancement of Colored People (NAACP). Work with the NAACP suited Evers, and in 1954 he became field secretary for the NAACP in Mississippi and moved his family to Jackson. Myrlie became her husband's secretary.

As Myrlie Evers and her husband dedicated themselves to their work, especially voter registration, death threats against Medgar, in particular, became commonplace. By this time, Myrlie and Medgar Evers had a family of their own. Their three young children, Darrell, Reena, and James, learned to fall to the floor of the house whenever they heard unusual noises at night. Everyone stayed away from the windows after dark. Both Evers and her husband felt that it was inevitable that someone would try to kill Medgar. Evers talked with her husband about moving to California and starting a new life. However, he was determined to continue working to change the oppressive conditions that blacks lived under in Mississippi, even if it might cost him his life.

Evers tried to ready herself for the moment when her worst nightmare would come true, but there was no way to prepare for it. Shortly after midnight on June 12, 1963, Evers and her children heard Medgar's car in the driveway as he returned home from an NAACP meeting. As he stepped out of his car, a shot rang out. The bullet passed through his body, continued through the living room window, and into the kitchen, where it lodged in the door of the refrigerator. When no more shots came, Evers and the children all ran out to see Medgar lying face down near the door. The children pleaded with him to get up, but their father did not respond; within an hour he was dead.

The murder weapon and its user, Byron de la Beckwith, were found. De la Beckwith was a segregationist and white supremacist. Evers-Williams remembers the day she testified at Beckwith's trial:

> The governor of Mississippi, Ross Barnett, walked in . . . and he paused and looked at me, turned, and went to Beckwith, shook his hand, slapped him on the shoulder, and sat down next to him. He was sending a clear signal to the jurors that his man was to be acquitted.[42]

The jury failed to reach a verdict. Though Beckwith was tried a second time, the jury again failed to reach a verdict. When the prosecutor decided not to retry the case, Beckwith went free.

Myrlie Evers and her children in a pilgrimage to Medgar Evers's grave in 1964.

A New Life and New Challenges

In 1964, following the second trial of her husband's accused murderer, Myrlie Evers began to pick up the pieces of her life. She moved her family to Claremont, California, near Los Angeles, where she enrolled at Pomona College, majoring in sociology. During the years of her studies, she supported herself with fees she earned for making public appearances on behalf of the NAACP. After graduation in 1968, she became the assistant director of the Claremont College system's Center for Education, which helped high school dropouts earn diplomas and go on to college.

Evers sought to continue the fight she and Medgar Evers had begun by running for political office. In 1970 she became the Democratic Party's candidate to represent California's Twenty-fourth Congressional District. The area that made up the District was heavily Republican. Her opponent, John Rousselot, was a member and former officer of the John Birch Society, an ultraconservative group. Although she lost, she was able to win 36 percent of the vote, which was more than any Democrat had gotten in the previous ten years. Myrlie Evers had served notice that she would be a force to be dealt with in coming years.

Recognizing that working in the corporate world was another key to bringing about positive change, in 1975 Evers became the national director for commu-nity affairs for the Atlantic Richfield Company (ARCO), one of the largest corporations in America. Her job was to co-ordinate programs that served communities in which the com-pany operated. For example, one program she worked on served meals to the poor and homeless in the Watts section of Los Angeles. Another project that Evers worked on was to broaden opportunities for women in the American work-force. As part of this effort, Evers developed a booklet about women in nontraditional jobs titled "Women at ARCO."

Byron de la Beckwith, the accused killer of Medgar Evers, as he is taken to the state mental hospital at Whitfield, Mississippi, for tests.

Evers also made changes in her personal life, becoming Myrlie Evers-Williams when she mar-ried fellow civil rights activist Walter Williams in 1976. In com-menting on her marriages dur-ing an interview with *Ebony* magazine's Marilyn Marshall, Evers-Williams indicated that "she has been 'blessed twice' in both of her marriages. . . . She admires her second husband for his ability to handle the pressure of being married to the widow of a martyr." [43]

Never one to sit still for long, by 1987 Evers-Williams was ready to try her hand at politics again. This time, she ran for a seat on the Los Angeles City Council. Again her campaign was

Remaining at the forefront of the civil rights struggle, Myrlie Evers (left) continued to fight for improvements in the lives of black Americans.

unsuccessful, but shortly after the election Los Angeles mayor Tom Bradley appointed Evers-Williams to the city's Board of Public Works.

On June 12, 1987, the Los Angeles City Council confirmed Evers-Williams's appointment, thereby making her the first black woman to serve on the Board of Public Works. In this position, she handled an operating budget of over $400 million, managed six thousand employees, and oversaw projects of the Bureaus of Sanitation, Street Maintenance, Street Lighting, Contract Administration, Engineering, and Accounting.

Justice for Medgar and Help for the NAACP

As the 1980s drew to a close, Evers-Williams and her husband decided to pursue a less hectic lifestyle than her Board of Public Works job allowed. Evers-Williams resigned, and the couple moved to the town of Bend, Oregon. However, just as they settled into the quiet life in Bend, news came from Mississippi about new evidence that could potentially be used to convict Medgar Evers's murderer.

A local newspaper in Jackson, the *Clarion-Ledger*, had begun investigating the possibility that there had been jury tampering by a secret organization known as the Mississippi Sovereignty Commission in the second trial of Byron de la Beckwith. Based on evidence discovered by the newspaper, Evers-Williams demanded the case be reopened. In the renewed investigation that followed, new witnesses came forward to testify that they had heard de la Beckwith brag about killing Medgar Evers. A new trial was ordered, and on February 5, 1994, Byron de la Beckwith was convicted of Medgar Evers's murder. Even though he was seventy-three years old, he was sentenced to life in prison. Seeing her husband's murderer convicted was a personal victory for Myrlie Evers-Williams.

At the NAACP

Evers-Williams took little time to savor this victory, however; there was more work to do. Soon after de la Beckwith's trial, Myrlie Evers-Williams was contacted by members of the NAACP to see if she would be interested in chairing the organization's board of directors. Although Evers-Williams was interested in running for the post, she found the decision difficult for several reasons. For one thing, her husband was seriously ill, and she wanted to spend as much time as possible with him. In addition, the NAACP itself was deeply divided over the close association that its executive director Benjamin Chavis maintained with Nation of Islam leader Louis Farrakhan. Many in the NAACP believed that Chavis's friendship with Farrakhan was inappropriate for the leader of a moderate mainstream organization like the NAACP, but others defended Chavis. Although Chavis had recently left his post, discord remained.

Finally, Evers-Williams decided she should run, and on February 7, 1995, she announced her candidacy, saying that the organization needed to address the issue of sexism (65 percent of the membership is female, but only eighteen of the sixty-four board members were women) and revitalize its membership. Victory was not certain. William F. Gibson, who held the post at the time, was still popular with many of the board's members despite charges that he had misused $1.4 million of the organization's funds. The race could not have been closer: Evers-Williams won by one vote.

In her new job, Evers-Williams set out to restore the reputation of the NAACP as a vocal and effective force for civil rights. Within days of her election, she set in motion a plan to pay off the nearly $4-million debt that had piled up under the leadership of her predecessors. To improve the handling of the organization's finances, she appointed a Wall Street financial manager, Frank Borges, to the post of treasurer.

To reverse the image of the NAACP as an old-fashioned organization that was out of touch with the times, she announced efforts to recruit more young members. The NAACP Youth Council and the NAACP Youth and College Division targeted black high schoolers and college students. As for addressing the role of women in the organization, Evers-Williams made it a priority to move women into key committee positions where they would participate in making major decisions.

Evers-Williams also felt that it was important for the NAACP to have a say in the federal government's plan for cutting social programs. Evers-Williams was alarmed that Congress was cutting programs that provided access for African Americans and other minorities to business opportunities. For instance, the minority-buyer incentive program, which encouraged minorities to enter the cable television industry and other areas of broadcasting, had been eliminated. Evers-Williams focused on doing research to support the need for programs that Congress wanted to cut. Knowing that members of Congress pay attention to voters, she encouraged the NAACP to put renewed emphasis on voter registration.

A New Look for the NAACP

Restoring the tarnished image of the NAACP was also a difficult challenge. In addition to the problems with debt and the personal hostility between individual members of the board of directors, many blacks no longer considered the NAACP to be the organization that stood up for their interests. By 1995, when African Americans were asked who was sticking up for them, they would often answer that it was Jesse Jackson or Louis Farrakhan. Evers-Williams was determined to return the NAACP to the status Georgia representative John R. Lewis recalled from his days as a civil rights worker: "When you said that the NAACP was coming to town . . . it meant that you were going to get some support. If something happened to you and people said they were going to call the NAACP, it was like manna from heaven."[44]

A major task in restoring the NAACP's health was to find someone who could fill the position of president and executive director, a post still vacant after the departure of Chavis in 1994. In February 1996 Evers-Williams brought Kweisi Mfume, a former congressman and one-time chair of the Congressional Black Caucus, in to fill the position. He agreed with Evers-Williams that the first order of business was setting up strict accountability for the organization's finances. One way to accomplish this goal was to streamline decision making. Rather than report to the NAACP's board of directors, Evers-Williams and Mfume arranged to report to a seventeen-member executive committee. This new organizational plan made it easier to obtain approval for new programs, which were desperately needed to help the NAACP's efforts at recruiting younger members.

Helping the NAACP to appeal to younger African Americans required the creation of some new programs that met the concerns of the twenty to thirty-five age group. Events like the Million Man March in October 1995 and 1997's Million Woman March had been designed to appeal to younger blacks, and the NAACP was conspicuous for its lack of participation. Evers-Williams commented to *Newsday* reporter John J. Giuffo, "The focus is going to be on program development. The NAACP has been criticized, and rightly so, for not being at the forefront of actions such as the Million Woman March and the Million Man March." [45]

Myrlie Evers-Williams waves to her supporters after she was elected chairperson of the board of directors of the NAACP in 1995.

Myrlie Evers-Williams retired from the NAACP in 1998, saying she felt she had succeeded in restoring the effectiveness of the organization.

Although her second husband died of cancer shortly after she became chair of the NAACP, Myrlie Evers-Williams refused to allow his loss to interfere with her work. Through her leadership and organizational efforts, the NAACP greatly reduced the financial debt and the internal quarreling that had crippled the organization. Her personal stature and credibility proved invaluable in restoring the effectiveness of the nation's oldest black civil rights organization.

In February 1998 Myrlie Evers-Williams announced that she would not seek a fourth one-year term as NAACP chair, saying that she had accomplished her goals there. Julian Bond, a former Georgia legislator, news commentator, and chairman of the NAACP publication *Crisis Magazine*, became the new chairman. Kweisi Mfume continues as president and executive director.

At age sixty-five, Evers-Williams remains a much-sought-after public speaker. Through her hard work, she made a name for herself separate from the work of her martyred first husband. Refusing to be satisfied with being what she describes as a professional widow, she says, "I know I wouldn't have had certain doors open to me if it hadn't been for Medgar. I also know if I hadn't had the intellect, I wouldn't be able to use it." [46] Myrlie Evers-Williams stands out as an example of what can be accomplished by embracing all that life sends, whether fortune or misfortune, and turning it into something useful.

NOTES

Chapter 1: A Brief History of the Civil Rights Movement

1. Martin Luther King Jr., "Letter from Birmingham Jail," April 16, 1963. http://power.pasco.lib.ll.us/mlk.htm/.

2. Cedric J. Robinson, *Black Movements in America*. New York: Routledge, 1997, p. 144.

3. Quoted in John Hope Franklin and Alfred A. Moss Jr., *From Slavery to Freedom: A History of African Americans*, 7th ed. New York: McGraw-Hill, 1994, p. 463.

Chapter 2: A. Philip Randolph: Father of the Civil Rights Movement

4. Quoted in Robinson, *Black Movements in America*, p. 120.

5. Paula F. Pfeffer, *A. Philip Randolph: Pioneer of the Civil Rights Movement*. Baton Rouge: Louisiana State University Press, 1990, pp. 10–11.

6. Quoted in Pfeffer, *A. Philip Randolph*, pp. 52–53.

7. Quoted in David L. Lewis, *King: A Biography*. Urbana: University of Illinois Press, 1978, pp. 218–19.

8. Quoted in Taylor Branch, *Parting the Waters: America in the King Years, 1954–1963*. New York: Simon and Schuster, 1988, p. 840.

Chapter 3: Thurgood Marshall: A Spokesman for Justice

9. Quoted in Carl T. Rowan, *Dream Makers, Dream Breakers: The World of Justice Thurgood Marshall*. Boston: Little, Brown, 1993, p. 38.

10. Quoted in Rowan, *Dream Makers, Dream Breakers*, p. 132.

11. Quoted in Rowan, *Dream Makers, Dream Breakers*, p. 132.

12. Quoted in Thurgood Marshall Webpage, "Biography of Thurgood Marshall." www.norfacad.pvt.k12.va.us/project/marshall/marshall.htm.

13. Quoted in Thurgood Marshall Webpage, "Biography of Thurgood Marshall."

Chapter 4: Martin Luther King Jr.: A Nonviolent Warrior

14. Quoted in BilLee Miller Webpage, "Martin Luther King Jr. Quotes," 1999. www.cptel.net/miller/BilLee/quotes/MLKJr.html.

15. Martin Luther King Jr., "Letter from Birmingham Jail," April 16, 1963. www.msstate.edu/Archives/History/USA/Afro-Amer/birmingham.king.

16. Martin Luther King Jr., "I Have a Dream," August 28, 1963. www.lib.grin.edu/resources/martin.html.

17. Martin Luther King Jr., "Nobel Prize Acceptance Speech," 1964. www.angelfire.com/tx/mlkingjr/nob/html.

18. Quoted in Lewis, *King*, pp. 218–19.

19. Quoted in BilLee Miller Webpage, "Martin Luther King Jr. Quotes."

Chapter 5: Malcolm X: A Voice of Anger

20. Quoted in Elke's Homepage, "Malcolm X Quotations," speech before the Militant Labor Forum, May 29, 1964. www.unix-ag.uni-kl.de/~moritz/malcolm.html.

21. Alex Haley and Malcolm X, *The Autobiography of Malcolm X*. New York: Ballantine Books, 1973, p. 242.

22. Quoted in Lewis, *King*, p. 206.

23. Haley and Malcolm X, *The Autobiography of Malcolm X*, p. 301.

24. Quoted in Elke's Homepage, "Malcolm X Quotations," interview with Louis Lomax, April 4, 1964. www.unix-ag.uni-kl.de/~moritz/malcolm.html.

25. Quoted in Patricia Robinson, "Malcolm X: Our Revolutionary Son and Brother," *New York Times*, February 22, 1966. www.unix-ag.uni-kl.de/~moritz/malcolm.html.

26. Quoted in *Chicago Defender*, November 28, 1962. www.unix-ag.uni-kl.de/~moritz/malcolm.html.

Chapter 6: Fannie Lou Hamer: An Everyday Heroine

27. Quoted in Kay Mills, *This Little Light of Mine: The Life of Fannie Lou Hamer*. New York: Dutton, 1993, p. 123.

28. Quoted in Woman a Week Archives, "Fannie Lou Townsend Hamer." http://members.aol.com/taylorteri/hamer/html.

29. Quoted in Pilgrim New Media, "Fannie Lou Hamer." www.plgrm.com/history/women/H/Fannie_Lou_Townsend_Hamer.HTM.

30. Quoted in Pilgrim New Media, "Fannie Lou Hamer."

31. Quoted in Pilgrim New Media, "Fannie Lou Hamer."

Chapter 7: Jesse Jackson: Preacher and Politician

32. Quoted in Troost Communication Academy, "Re: The Communicators to Rev. Jesse Jackson," September 21, 1995. http://llsn.bbn.com/resources/bts/jackson/subject.html.

33. Quoted Frontline, "The Pilgrimage of Jesse Jackson," interview with biographer Marshall Frady, 1996. http://pbs.org/wgbh/pages/frontline/jesse/fradyint.html.

34. Quoted in Frontline, "The Pilgrimage of Jesse Jackson," interview with Jackie Jackson, 1998. http://pbs.org/wgbh/pages/frontline/jesse/interviews/jackie.html.

35. Quoted in Frontline, "The Pilgrimage of Jesse Jackson," interview with biographer Marshall Frady.

36. Jesse Jackson, "Address Before the Democratic National Convention," July 18, 1984. http://pbs.org/wgbh/pages/frontline/jesse/speeches/jesse84speech.html.

37. Quoted in Elizabeth Colton, *The Jackson Phenomenon: The Man, the Power, the Message.* New York: Doubleday, 1989, p. 272.

38. Jesse Jackson, "You Do Not Stand Alone," July 14, 1992. http://metalab.unc.edu/pub/docs/speeches/demo-conv/jjackson.txt/.

39. Quoted in Cyber Nation, Quotation Center, "Jesse Jackson." www.cyber-nation.com/victory/quotations/authors/quotes_jackson_jesse.html.

Chapter 8: Myrlie Evers-Williams: A New Kind of Leader

40. Myrlie Evers-Williams, "Dear Danny," U.S. News Online, 1998. www.usnews.com/news/evers.htm.

41. Evers-Williams, "Dear Danny."

42. Quoted in Claudia Dreifus, "The Widow Gets Her Verdict," *New York Times Magazine,* November 27, 1994, p. 69.

43. Quoted in Marilyn Marshall, "Myrlie Evers-Williams Remembers: Twenty-five Years After Assassination of Civil Rights Leader," *Ebony,* June 1988, p. 114.

44. Quoted in Eric Smith, "The Great Black Hope," *Black Enterprise,* February 1996, p. 150.

45. Quoted in John J. Giuffo, "Work Yet to Be Done," *Newsday,* January 17, 1998. www.newsday.com/mainnews/rnmi0alm.htm.

46. Quoted in Dreifus, "The Widow Gets Her Verdict," p. 69.

For Further Reading

Books

Lisa Aldred, *Thurgood Marshall: Supreme Court Justice.* New York: Chelsea House, 1990. A biography with bibliographical references and a chronology.

Mark Davies, *Marcolm X.* Englewood Cliffs, NJ: Silver Burdett, 1990. A biography with a bibliography, chronology, and comparative timeline.

Sally Hanley, *A. Philip Randolph: Labor Leader.* New York: Chelsea House, 1989. A biography focused on Randolph's labor-union activities.

James Haskins, *I Have a Dream: The Life and Words of Martin Luther King Jr.* Brookfield, CT: Millbrook, 1992. A biography in photos and excerpts from famous speeches.

———, *The Life and Death of Martin Luther King Jr.* New York: William Morrow, 1977. A biography with photos.

Della Rowland, *Martin Luther King Jr.: The Dream of Peaceful Revolution.* Englewood Cliffs, NJ: Silver Burdett, 1990. A biography with bibliographical references, a chronology, and a comparative timeline.

David Rubel, *Fannie Lou Hamer: From Sharecropping to Politics.* Englewood Cliffs, NJ: Silver Burdett, 1990. A biography with bibliographical references, a chronology, and a comparative timeline.

William Strickland and Cheryll Greene, *Malcolm X: Make It Plain.* New York: Viking, 1994. Contains oral history and photos.

Brenda Wilkinson, *Jesse Jackson: Still Fighting for the Dream.* Englewood Cliffs, NJ: Silver Burdett, 1990. A biography with bibliographical references, a chronology, and a comparative timeline.

Sarah Wright, *A. Philip Randolph: Integration in the Work Place.* Englewood Cliffs, NJ: Silver Burdett, 1990. A biography with bibliographical references, a chronology, and a comparative timeline.

Encyclopedia

Alton Hornsby Jr., *Chronology of African-American History: Significant Events and People from 1619 to the Present.* Detroit: Gale Research, 1991. A reference book with photos and illustrations.

Websites

Fannie Lou Hamer *(*www.plgrm.com/history/women/H/Fannie_Lou_ Townsend_Hamer.HTM). This site provides a biography of Hamer and links to biographies of other famous American women.

Martin Luther King Jr. (http://power.pasco.lib.ll.us/mlk.htm/). Offers information on King's life, including texts of several of his famous speeches.

Malcolm X (www.unix-ag.uni-kl.de/·moritz/malcolm.html). Extensive quotations of Malcolm X from a variety of books, speeches, and articles.

Thurgood Marshall *(*www.aorfacad.pvt.k12.va.us/project/marshall/ laterlif.htm). Provides a biography of Thurgood Marshall with quotes.

WORKS CONSULTED

Books

Jervis B. Anderson, *A. Philip Randolph: A Biographical Portrait.* New York: Harcourt Brace Jovanovich, 1972. Offers an in-depth biography of A. Philip Randolph.

Taylor Branch, *Parting the Waters: America in the King Years, 1954–1963.* New York: Simon and Schuster, 1988. Comprehensive coverage of the civil rights movement from the Supreme Court school desegregation order through the March on Washington.

Elizabeth Colton, *The Jackson Phenomenon: The Man, the Power, the Message.* New York: Doubleday, 1989. Focuses on Jesse Jackson's presidential campaign of 1988.

John Hope Franklin and Alfred A. Moss Jr., *From Slavery to Freedom: A History of African Americans.* 7th ed. New York: McGraw-Hill, 1994. A survey of four hundred years of African American history.

Peter Goldman, *The Death and Life of Malcolm X.* Chicago: University of Chicago Press, 1979. Concentrates on Malcolm X's last days and his relationship with the Nation of Islam.

Alex Haley and Malcolm X, *The Autobiography of Malcolm X.* New York: Ballantine Books, 1973. The story of Malcolm X's life as told to Alex Haley by Malcolm X.

David L. Lewis, *King: A Biography.* Urbana: University of Illinois Press, 1978. An in-depth biography emphasizing details of King's civil rights activities.

Kay Mills, *This Little Light of Mine: The Life of Fannie Lou Hamer.* New York: Dutton, 1993. A biography developed from interviews with Hamer.

Paula F. Pfeffer, *A. Philip Randolph: Pioneer of the Civil Rights Movement.* Baton Rouge: Louisiana State University Press, 1990. Emphasizes Randolph's leadership in civil rights activities before the civil rights movement.

Barbara Reynolds, *Jesse Jackson: The Man, the Movement, the Myth.* Chicago: Nelson-Hill, 1975. Coverage of Jesse Jackson in the days of PUSH and his early career as an activist.

Cedric J. Robinson, *Black Movements in America.* New York: Routledge, 1997. A scholarly historical survey of organized activities by African Americans to gain freedom and civil rights.

Carl T. Rowan, *Dream Makers, Dream Breakers: The World of Justice Thurgood Marshall.* Boston: Little, Brown, 1993. A biography of Marshall based on interviews by journalist Rowan.

Juan Williams, *Eyes on the Prize: America's Civil Rights Years, 1954–1965.* New York: Viking, 1987. In-depth coverage of the civil rights movement and companion piece to the PBS documentary series by the same name.

Periodical

Zita Allen, "Myrlie Victorious," *Public Employees Press*, August 23, 1996.

Verena Dobnik, "Julian Bond New NAACP Chairman," *Seattle Times*, February 22, 1998.

Claudia Dreifus, "The Widow Gets Her Verdict," *New York Times Magazine*, November 27, 1994.

Marilyn Marshall, "Myrlie Evers-Williams Remembers: Twenty-five Years After Assassination of Civil Rights Leader," *Ebony*, June 1988.

Jill Petty, "Myrlie Evers-Williams," *Ms.*, January/February 1996.

Eric Smith, "The Great Black Hope," *Black Enterprise*, February 1996.

Internet Sources

BilLee Miller Webpage, "Martin Luther King Jr. Quotes," 1999. www.cp-tel.net/miller/BilLee/quotes/MLKJr.html.

Chicago Defender, November 28, 1962. www.unix-ag.uni-kl.de/~moritz/malcolm.html.

Cyber Nation, Quotation Center, "Jesse Jackson." www.cyber-nation.com/victory/quotations/authors/quotes_jackson_jesse.html.

Elke's Homepage, "Malcolm X Quotations," interview with Louis Lomax, April 4, 1964. www.unix-ag.uni-kl.de/~moritz/malcolm.html.

———, "Malcolm X Quotations," speech before the Militant Labor Forum, May 29, 1964. www.unix-ag.uni-kl.de/~moritz/malcolm.html.

Myrlie Evers-Williams, "Dear Danny," U.S. News Online, 1998. www.usnews.com/usnews/news/evers.htm.

Frontline, "The Pilgrimage of Jesse Jackson," interview with biographer Marshall Frady, 1996. http://pbs.org/wgbh/pages/frontline/jesse/fradyint.html.

———, "The Pilgrimage of Jesse Jackson," interview with Jackie Jackson, 1998. http://pbs.org/wgbh/pages/frontline/jesse/interviews/jackie.html.

John J. Giuffo, "Work Yet to Be Done," *Newsday*, January 17, 1998. www.newsday.com/mainnews/rnmi0alm.htm.

Jesse Jackson, "Address Before the Democratic National Convention," July 18, 1984. http://pbs.org/wgbh/pages/frontline/jesse/speeches/jesse84speech.html.

———, "You Do Not Stand Alone," July 14, 1992. http://metalab.unc.edu/pub/docs/speeches/demo-conv/jjackson.txt/.

Martin Luther King Jr., "I Have a Dream," August 28, 1963. www.lib.grin.edu/resources/martin.html.

———, "Letter from Birmingham Jail," April 16, 1963. http://power.pasco.lib.ll.us/mlk.htm/.

———, "Letter from Birmingham Jail," April 16, 1963. www.msstate.edu/Archives/History/USA/Afro-Amer/birmingham.king.

———, "Nobel Prize Acceptance Speech," 1964. www.angelfire.com/tx/mlkingjr/nob/html.

Pilgrim New Media, "Fannie Lou Hamer." www.plgrm.com/history/women/H/Fannie_Lou_Townsend_Hamer.HTM.

Patricia Robinson, "Malcolm X: Our Revolutionary Son and Brother," *New York Times*, February 22, 1966. www.unix-ag.uni-kl.de/~moritz/malcolm.html.

Thurgood Marshall Webpage, "Biography of Thurgood Marshall." www.norfacad. pvt.k12.va.us/project/marshall/marshall.htm.

Troost Communication Academy, "Re: The Communicators to Rev. Jesse Jackson," September 21, 1995. http://llsn.bbn.com/resources/bts/jackson/subject.html.

Woman a Week Archives, "Fannie Lou Townsend Hamer." http://members.aol.com/ taylorteri/hamer/html.

INDEX

PICTURE CREDITS

ABOUT THE AUTHOR

Marjorie Vernell grew up in Omaha, Nebraska, during the years of the civil rights movement. As an African American adolescent, she was much influenced by the changes that the movement fostered, including the expanded possibilities that blacks had for participating fully in American society and in the world.

She received her Bachelor of Arts degree from the University of Toronto in Canada and her Masters of Arts degree from San Francisco State University. After having spent many years teaching Spanish and English to high school students, she began working with adult learners.

Ms. Vernell has lived in Canada, Mexico, and France. She currently teaches in the Department of Writing and Communication at National University in San Diego.